GARLAND STUDIES IN

THE HISTORY OF AMERICAN LABOR

edited by

STUART BRUCHEY
UNIVERSITY OF MAINE

A GARLAND SERIES

SINGLE OLDER WOMEN IN THE WORKFORCE

By Necessity, or Choice?

JENNIFER KANE COPLON

GARLAND PUBLISHING, Inc.
New York & London / 1997

Library of Congress Cataloging-in-Publication Data

Coplon, Jennifer K., 1945–
    Single older women in the workforce : by necessity, or
choice? / Jennifer Kane Coplon.
          p.   cm. — (Garland studies in the history of American
labor)
    Revision of the author's thesis (Ph. D.)—Brandeis University,
1994.
    Includes bibliographical references and index.
    ISBN 0-8153-2837-0 (alk. paper)
    1. Middle aged women—Employment—United States.
2. Single women—Employment—United States. 3. Age and
employment—United States. I. Title. II. Series.
HD6056.2.U6C67 1997
331.3'98'0820973—dc21
                                                            97-9289

Printed on acid-free, 250-year-life paper
Manufactured in the United States of America

Contents

List of Tables

ix

List of Figures

Preface

Unlike men and married women, single women over age 54 generally cannot look forward to retirement free of economic worry. For these women, Social Security income does not necessarily serve as a safety net against poverty, because of their aggregate record of unemployment, erratic work histories, low paying jobs, and low or no pensions or savings for retirement. Using data from a large national study, the author identifies this often ignored segment of the population.

Those women who work more hours are more likely to be financially secure. Divorced are more likely than widowed older women to work full time. "Younger" older women are also more likely to work full time. In contrast, the level of education, race, living arrangements, and regional location are not necessarily related to the likelihood of full-time work. Single older women in technical, sales, service, or administrative support jobs are more likey to work part time, often not by choice, whereas professional/managerial women or operators/fabricators voluntarily work full time. What usually comes with full-time work—and not with part-time work—is employer-paid health insurance.

A surprising proportion (12 percent) of single older women work after age 70, almost the same percent who work between ages 62 and 64. One-quarter of these women work full-time. Their wages and incomes are lowest, but they have more non-earned income, mostly Social Security.

The author recommends various employment policies to encourage single older women to remain in the workforce. She also proposes reforms that offer to older women a financial choice not to work, similar to the option available to older men.

Acknowledgments

My study would never have been possible without the untiring support of my late husband, Fred Coplon. Fred was always available when I needed him and believed wholeheartedly in me. My sadness is that he is not here to enjoy the fruits of my—and his—labor.

I am also appreciative of my now grown daughters, Gina and Stephanie, who at first tolerated and later became proud of my perserverance in completing this seemingly endless "project." My late parents, Pearl and James Kane, also deserve my heartfelt thanks. They raised me with the confidence that I could attain anything that I really wanted if I was willing to work hard for it.

Also, I am very grateful to the untiring academic guidance of Bill Crown, Janet Giele, Hilda Kahne, and Jim Schulz, and the caring computer and editorial support of Bob Frank. Last but not least, my mother-in-law, Rose Coplon, was an admirable role model of the single older working woman; she continued to work full time as a legal secretary until age 73 when her law firm closed.

Single Older Women
in the Workforce

Chapter I

Description of Study

INTRODUCTION

This is a study of contemporary single women (widowed, divorced, separated, and never married) ages 55 and older who are working full time and part time (i.e., fewer than 35 hours per week). Subgroups of these women, particularly those working less than and those working more than half time, are compared. Also, women with similar demographic, labor force, and income characteristics, yet working full time, are analyzed so as to determine any significant differences between the full-time and the part-time workers. As a comparison group, non-working women with similar demographic profiles are researched in order to determine significant economic differences between the working and non-working samples.

Historically, statistical data have compared full-time workers to part-timers—that is, those working 35 hours or more to those working fewer hours. Part-time workers, regardless of hours of work per week, have been lumped together as one category. The data about part-time workers include such demographic factors as age, sex, race, occupation, industry, and education. However, the variable of "hours of work" has been essentially unexplored. Surely the older person, and more specifically for the purposes of this research, the 55+ year old single woman, who works less than half time per week, presents a different profile from the 18+ hour-a-week older single woman. The most obvious difference, of course, is weekly pay, but older single women who work varying degrees of part time, may differ significantly on other measures as well: age, marital status, education, race, household composition, regional location, occupation, employee benefits (health insurance and pension coverage), company type (public or private), work site size, reason for working part time (voluntary or involuntary), hourly wage, non-market income/assets, and household wealth. Their motivation to work 10 hours versus 20 to 30 hours, for example, may relate partly to these variables as well as to other variables, such as psychological well being that is not being directly analyzed in this study. And, among these variables to be explored, some factors may explain more fully than others the relationship between specific demographic, income, and labor force characteristics of single women 55+ and the extent of their labor force participation—that is, their "choice" in the number of their weekly working hours.

For women in general throughout the life cycle, alternative work schedules, including flexitime, compressed work weeks, job sharing, and part-time jobs, are particularly attractive employment choices as they bear and rear children and as they continue in the role of caregivers to aging spouses and relatives and dependent adult children. Older workers often have the added consideration of health constraints and of desiring more leisure over work when making employment decisions.

Given increased longevity of elders in general and, more specifically, of women outliving men, many women over time are left in the position of having to support themselves financially due to widowhood, divorce, separation, or never having been married. With the eventuality of being alone in their later years, these women may need to work as long as possible in order to stave off poverty. According to a report by the Villers Foundation, women 85 years of age and older have a poverty rate of 19.7 percent, and elderly black women living alone have an astounding poverty rate of 54.5 percent (*On the Other Side of Easy Street*, 1987).

Although Social Security benefits have drastically reduced poverty among elders as a group, many aged single women are still prone to poverty. They have on average limited earnings histories and resulting low Social Security benefits based on their individual earnings, minimal non-market income, and few pensions. Private and public employment policies and practices both need to include ways of making possible labor force participation among older women. Enhancing part-time job options is one viable means of achieving that goal. Studying actual work behavior in terms of the number of work hours per week will contribute to a better understanding of what demographic and economic variables influence working hours. With more effective predictive information, part-time work can be better designed to meet the needs of this group.

For example, the results of this analysis will provide new data that could be used to shape reforms in Social Security legislation: in liberalizing or eliminating the earnings test (so that retirees are not penalized so stringently for working more hours so as to have more pay); in designing retirement alternatives (such as extending employment through creative transitions from full-time to part-time employment); in creating job opportunities for older women (based upon more precise descriptions of their characteristics and their possible economic motivations for working part time); and in developing programs and policies that promote continuation or return of older single women to the part-time labor force. This expanded part-time workforce would provide not only additional income to older women but also increased payroll and income tax dollars to society. In addition, as earnings keep more single older women above the poverty line, there would be less of a drain on other government supports such as Supplemental Security Income, Medicaid, Food Stamps, and housing allowances.

SOCIAL SIGNIFICANCE OF THE PROBLEM

The economic security of older workers is of increasing concern to policy makers in both the public and private sector. As older people prepare financially for their extended futures on relatively fixed incomes, continuing to work beyond traditional retirement ages becomes more crucial, particularly for those whose financial futures are not secure. For many individuals the need to work may include factors other than economic: psychological and social benefits, expected and realized, such as connectedness to the society at large, as well as increased self esteem and self worth, and decreased depression and loneliness. From a societal perspective and according to Americans for Generational Equity, the need to extend labor force participation arises from predicted future economic conditions: an increasing labor shortage and a heightened "burden" on Social Security and other pensions (Longman, 1985). Although the total dependency ratio will be lower in the future than it was in the 1950's and 1960's because of decreasing births and an increasing work population, that ratio of non-working elders to the total number of workers will only expand. The intergenerational "advocates" contend that the dwindling working population will be increasingly responsible for supporting the Social Security benefits of the expanding numbers of retired elders. Consequently, policy makers ought to be thinking creatively about strategies for encouraging the older worker to remain in or return to the workforce. These strategies may be positive or negative in nature: employment incentives, on the one hand, and retirement disincentives on the other (Crown, 1989).

Older people who work are much less likely to be poor than those who do not. Although attention to older workers in general is of growing importance, women among this group are particularly at risk economically because of their typically limited work histories, poor paying jobs, and minimal employee benefits. And, among these women those who are single—and living alone—are most at risk with fewest resources from which to draw or to share.

Older single women as an aggregate, defined for the purposes of this study as 55 and older and including all categories of singlehood (never married, widowed, divorced, and separated), are America's largest most economically vulnerable population (Warlick, 1985; *On the Other Side of Easy Street*, 1987). Fifteen percent of women over 65 (2.4 million) live in poverty, slightly higher than the national average. At age 65 plus, their median incomes in 1983 were just over half those of older men—$6425 versus $11,544, with $5061 as the poverty line for a single person in 1983 (Loth, 1986). They are more than twice as likely as men to live in poverty, partly because women tend to outlive men by an average of 7 years and by at least 4 additional years after age 65: to age 83 versus 79 on average (Crown, 1985; Kahne, 1985; Schulz, 1988).

In addition to increased longevity, lower wages, intermittent labor force attachment, and occupational segregation have contributed to the lack of economic resources of older women. They have lower benefits than men and younger women from public and private pensions as well as meager non-market assets. As a result, they are more likely to require additional government support in the form of SSI, Medicaid, and other types of public assistance (Kahne, 1985; Sohn, 1988). And, when these older women are single and have no one else to rely on for augmenting their often bare resources or for sharing financial costs, many of these women are substantially more likely to be at risk.

In order to determine more precisely the roots of poverty, it is important to break down the aggregate of single older women into more specific subgroups. Based upon marital status, widows who are covered by a deceased spouse's Social Security may be perhaps the least disadvantaged subset of single older women as compared to divorced and never married women. They comprise 24 percent of all non-married women entering retirement each year ("Women and Social Security," 1985). However, they, too, suffer economic hardship as they live on a benefit schedule that reflects spouses' wage levels (even with periodic cost of living adjustments) more than living cost increases and inflation. Consequently, these women who live longer on these relatively fixed incomes, must reduce their standard of living.

Also, most current widows stop receiving a retired spouse's private pension at the time of his death. There may be a few exceptions among women whose husbands died following the 1986 implementation of the 1984 Retirement Equity Act that mandates automatic joint survivor annuity insurance unless waived by both spouses in writing. However, widows most at risk economically are those whose husbands had no pensions (Burkhauser, 1988).

According to the New Beneficiary Survey of 1982, never married (5 percent of the one-third non-married women entering retirement) and divorced/separated women (7 percent of this population) represent a rapidly rising number of women who are even more vulnerable than widows in their later years. These women whose own earnings generally determine the amount of their Social Security benefits (except for the relatively few who are receiving benefits as divorced wives), have smaller government pensions than men ($420 versus $460 per month in 1982), higher earnings and fewer total assets than widows, even if their Social Security benefits alone are higher than widows' ("Women and Social Security," 1985). Even with continuous work histories, single women have generally held jobs in firms that do not offer private pensions (Schofield, 1984).

Divorced women with children have even fewer economic resources; their work histories have been typically sporadic and their resulting career opportunities limited as they have taken time out of the labor force for childrearing (O'Rand and Henretta, 1982). In other words, older divorced women often face double jeopardy: they have neither economic security from a spouse (dead or alive) nor established resources of their own from continuous labor force attachment. Unless their marriages last at least 10 years, they have no financial protection under former spouses' Social Security. Even then, payments or benefits— at only 50 percent of ex-husbands' entitlements (unless they receive higher benefits based on their own earnings histories)—do not begin until the divorced husband reaches 62 and has chosen to retire. Given these restrictive conditions, many divorced women prefer receipt of benefits based upon their own earnings, which are often lower than those of single women or men with longer and stronger work histories. After many years of full-time homemaking, these women become "displaced" (Flaim and Sehgal, 1985), have few current job-related skills, limited job opportunities, and very scary economic futures.

In addition to marital status, race is a major determinant of single older women's economic vulnerability. Older minority women, with blacks as the largest group, are most at risk. Although older black women have traditionally had longer work histories than many white women, their jobs have been more menial, less stable, and poorer paying (Bowen and Finegan, 1969; Brody, 1976; Brown, 1988; Cain, 1976; Kaplan, 1984). Single parenthood has been more prevalent in minority than in Caucasian communities. Therefore, women of color have been less able to rely on the resources of spouses, many of whom have suffered long stretches of unemployment related to racial discrimination and lack of job opportunities and job training.

There are other demographic variables that affect the economic status of single older women. Years of education is highly correlated with occupation and income level. Working women with at least a high school education have more job opportunities and career advancements. However, older women today generally are not so well educated as younger women; their early years occurred during the Depression when education was less affordable and, perhaps, less valued. Also, the role of women was different at that point in history; most older women did not grow up with equal opportunity for men and women in the areas of both education and work as a social norm and a legal responsibility. The widely held belief was that women's primary role as adults was as wives and mothers. Women were expected to get married, have children, and then stay home in order to fully care for the family and the home. While some of these older women pursued a college education, it was generally not done for the purposes of securing a job or a profession. Rather, college, especially the women's college, according to the 1984-87 Study of Life Course Patterns and Well-Being in Educated Women, was often considered to be like a finishing school for women of this cohort, (certainly drastically changing with future cohorts), and a socially acceptable way of meeting desirable men for marriage (Giele and Gilfus, 1990). In other words, education for women in the years preceding World War II was not usually valued as a stepping stone to better jobs. Unfortunately, these women, who in their later years find that they need to work for economic reasons, have neither adequate education nor work histories that can assist in obtaining jobs other than menial ones.

Age works against older workers as well, though perhaps no more for women than for men. But together with the other factors described above, it jeopardizes even more women's chances of finding work. Age discrimination does exist, regardless of the removal of the national mandatory retirement law in 1986 (Herz and Rones, 1989; Schuster and Miller, 1984; Schuster and Kaspin, 1987; Weiss, 1984; U.S. Department of Labor, 1980). Myths about older workers persist (*Workers Over 50*, 1986; Sandell, 1987; Scott and Brudney, 1987). Elderly workers are perceived as less productive, more prone to sickness and accidents, inflexible, obsolete and less retrainable, and generally more costly to employers. Age discrimination works against older workers being hired as well as being retained. Circumventing the Age Discrimination in Employment Act (ADEA) of 1978 has been successful and lawful through voluntary early retirement packages, considered "golden handshakes" by some and "shoves" by others (Gorov, 1985). As conflicted as early retirees may feel about these plans, they have offered a certain degree of financial security—though mainly to men. Older women are least likely to hold high-salaried jobs eligible for such plans.

Company closures and mergers as well as downsizing due to economic necessity have cost many employees their jobs. The National Association of Working Women describes older workers as "shock absorbers" (Golden, 1987, pp. iii, 29) in this changing, more internationally competitive economy. When workers lose good jobs in their late forties/early fifties, they are less likely to refind comparable jobs (Scott and Brudney, 1987). As a result, they suffer extended periods of unemployment and significant cuts in salary when they are re-employed. Women with less employment seniority, due to intermittent work histories or a delayed return to work as displaced homemakers, are most vulnerable to losing their jobs during economically hard times. Thus, older women, often displaced from their homes because of widowhood, separation, divorce, or long-term disability of a spouse, are not able to find work. And, their economic vulnerability is exacerbated when, having a job, they lose it and cannot find other work. They then often become discouraged workers and eventually drop out of the job market—trapped in poverty and forced to rely on government programs for income support.

Segments of the population 65+ are in great risk of being in poverty. Most people over 65 are women, and the percentage grows with age: 59 percent of those over 65 and 62 percent over 75. Single older women are particularly at risk; they comprise 72 percent of poor people age 65+. Minority women also face significant hardship; 40 percent age 65+ live in poverty.

This wage discrimination that women and minorities suffer throughout their work lives severely impacts their retirement incomes. Few women, particularly those in private industry without unions, have private pensions. Sales and service industries, where women's jobs are primarily concentrated, have the fewest pension plans. Because of their discontinuous work patterns, brought about by leaving the workforce to rear children, older women have not been in jobs long enough to be eligible for pension vesting, especially with the traditional cliff vesting at ten years, which was typical of many companies until the 1986 change in the ERISA law that has lowered both the minimal age of eligibility and the required years on the job for vesting.

Those few eligible for vesting, however, are entitled to limited pension benefits based upon their low-paying jobs and restricted years of service. Another problem for the minority of women who are eligible for private pensions is the integrated plan, typical of many non-union, low-paying industries where women tend to work in numbers. In this type of plan, the employer subtracts a portion of the Social Security earnings from the accrued pension benefits in calculating the monthly pension amount. Because Social Security is progressive, paying a higher percentage to those with lower incomes, integration has a leveling effect on total pension replacement rates by taking away a greater percentage from lower-income workers. (The Tax Reform Act of 1986, implemented beginning in 1989, targets average earnings rather than Social Security benefits in reducing pension benefits. However, the end result on workers at various income levels remains the same.)

Given that private pension benefits are non-existent or minimal for most women as well as fixed in dollar amount over time (with infrequent or no cost of living adjustments), few women could survive on private pension benefits alone. Social Security benefits account for 85 percent of the income of the average single older woman (U.S. Department of Labor, 1980). Although originally designed as a base, Social Security is the only source of income for 60 percent of older women.

In addition to sex, single older women working part time have many strikes against them: marital status, longevity, age, limited education and work histories, obsolete job skills, low paying jobs and no pensions. Many have the ability, motivation and economic need to continue working, but full-time work may not be a viable alternative for a number of reasons: (1) they may be tired of tedious jobs and long for leisure time; (2) they may have chronic deterring health problems (Kingson, 1979); (3) they may experience job obsolescence with declining industries and new employment technologies; (4) they may have caregiving responsibilities for spouses or elder parents (Gibeau, 1986); (5) they may have nothing to gain economically from remaining full time in the labor force—and even something to lose in the form of a 50 percent penalty on Social Security benefits that surpass the earnings limitation (having changed to 33 percent in 1990) and a less-than-actuarially fair credit of 3 percent per year prior to 1987 for delaying Social Security entitlements, increasing gradually to 8 percent by 2004 (Herz and Rones, 1989); (6) they may not find jobs because of persistent age discrimination and negative attitudes about older workers (Weiss, 1984; *On the Other Side of Easy Street*, 1987; Herz and Rones, 1989); (7) they may be encouraged to retire in order to avoid foregone pension benefits and implicit earnings taxes (Herz and Rones, 1989); (8) they may prefer the tradeoff of more leisure for less work as they grow older, particularly if they have sufficient income (Crown, Mutschler, and Leavitt, 1987; Schulz, 1988); and (9) they may reject poorly paying part-time jobs without benefits following retirement (Kahne, 1985; Herz and Rones, 1989).

Part-time employment can be a "workable" compromise between full retirement and full-time work (Future of Older Workers in America, 1984). It is an effective strategy for gradually phasing in retirement: to test out a life style without full-time employment and to explore ways of expanding leisure time pursuits. Part-time work may be a particularly appealing choice for physically able older workers who want to supplement their relatively fixed income of pension, savings, and other assets. Also, part-time work offers psychological benefits in the form of social status, life direction, and role definition. Women, in particular, continue to enjoy the social support and comraderie that work colleagues provide (Markson, 1983).

Although a majority of respondents from the 1981 National Council on Aging/Louis Harris Survey have indicated an interest in part-time work as a phase-in to full retirement (Shephard & Montovani, 1982), the reality is that most workers end up retiring suddenly, not gradually. The question remains as to why this happens. One reason may be management problems concerning pension eligibility. Another factor may be the reduction of private pension benefits when pre-retirement hours and income are decreased. In addition to these issues, are there other reasons for sudden retirement? Are phased retirement jobs unavailable? In one study of women following retirement, scarcer job opportunities, part time included, was cited as the reason for not working (Duke University Center on Aging, 1986). And, are there other equally significant reasons for not working part time following retirement or in place of retirement: the taste for full leisure over work, stringent economic penalties to Social Security benefits for working beyond a bare income minimum, financial disincentives such as an insufficient annual tax credit for delaying retirement, and unappealing post-retirement jobs at low wages without benefits and with menial responsibilities (Kahne, 1985)?

CONCLUSION

Given the recent boom in part-time and contingent jobs, there has probably never been a better time to research factors that influence part-time employment of older workers. This surge in part-time jobs, while driven more by employer demand than by the preference of workers in general (Ehrenberg, et al., 1986; Golden, 1987), does afford new opportunities and choices for older workers. Although this study examines older women in 1984, the findings have relevance for current trends in part-time employment.

Additional information about the characteristics of these single older women will contribute to more effective and timely employment policies and practices. With public and private sector reforms that encourage their labor force participation, these women would have more options to work. The "real" choice of working—at jobs that include adequate pay, benefits, and flexibility of hours—serves to benefit society as well, since increased labor force participation of older workers reduces government expenses (e.g., Social Security and SSI) and raises government income through payroll taxes.

Chapter II

Literature Review

INTRODUCTION: REASONS FOR STUDY

Although the issues of older workers and part-time workers have been of growing concern to researchers, policy analysts, and practitioners, the combined area regarding part-time versus full-time employment of older workers has received relatively little research attention. Women workers in this age category have been particularly neglected. Besides, part-time workers as a whole are usually compared to full-time workers in terms of such characteristics as hourly pay, job/industry classification, age, race, sex, and education and described as aggregate groups. The distinct subgroups among part-time workers, specifically those working either less than half time or more than half time, have been essentially overlooked as they may vary according to demographics, employment, and income characteristics. Consequently, this chapter reviews the literature that does exist about part-time employment and older workers as an aggregate category, with special attention to single older women. The gaps in existing research that this study attempts to reduce include a definition of "older" as 60 or 65 rather than 55; consideration of part-time work as one large category of labor force attachment rather than less than half time and more than half time as two separate categories; the impact of part-time employment on all workers rather than its effect on varying subgroups of workers, primarily single older women; and a focus on all older working women rather than solely on single older working women whose demographic, employment, and income profiles may differ from, for example, married women or non-working single women of this same age cohort.

From this ground work of what does and does not exist in the literature about these single older working women, a rationale is built for the importance of studying more closely this population that, as longevity increases, requires the attention of both the public and private sectors in formulating employment and social welfare policies that respond to their needs. Hence, the reasons for exploring the demographic, employment, and economic conditions of single older working women are clarified for the analysis that follows.

QUALITATIVE STUDIES

Much of the literature about older female part-time workers is descriptive, exploratory, and historical. Hilda Kahne (1985) has written a major treatise on the state of affairs for workers in part-time jobs, with particular emphasis on older women. She describes these women as exploited, underpaid, stuck in dead-end jobs, and often unprotected in terms of seniority or employee benefits. Part-time employment is especially responsive to the lifestyle of women with children, younger workers in school, and older workers phasing into retirement. Part-time employment is on the rise mostly in the expanding retail trade and service industries, where women have traditionally worked. Although Kahne describes the negative employment conditions of older and female workers, the main thrust of her book is to advocate "New Concept" part-time work that supports pay and employee benefits prorated to an equivalency with that accorded full-time jobs. "New Concept" part-time work, one might speculate, could motivate more people to work longer and thereby put less stress on public and private retirement programs and on supplemental security income (SSI) costs. As such, employees, employers, and society as a whole would stand to benefit from this approach.

Kahne (1993) has recently reassessed the problem of part-time work. Since the early 1990's about one-fifth of the non-agricultural labor force (20 million workers) have been working part time. Two-thirds of part-time jobs are filled by women, even though their representation in the civilian labor force is much less (43 percent). Of this number, there is a rapid rise in the contingent, involuntary workforce, responsible for half the new jobs in 1992.

However, Kahne contends that there is a viable role for part-time work. Changes in the labor market, specifically from a production to a service economy, has opened up many part-time jobs where there are great variations in weekly workloads and a resulting need for a flexible labor force. Also, changes in family structures, specifically the rise in two-worker families as well as in poor single mother families with young children in need of child care, often limit the availability of women for full-time jobs until children are school-age. Kahne advocates for "variable hour scheduled jobs" (p. 26) that are responsive to both the labor market and family needs. These jobs may be either part time or full time with standards equivalent to full time, including an emphasis on job training. As a result, companies and employees both serve to gain in terms of productivity, flexibility, and earnings.

Tilly (1991), on the other hand, focuses on the involuntary nature of part-time work, driven by employer demand for a flexible and low paying workforce. Most part-time jobs (in service industries) are secondary, defined as low paying, unskilled, unstable, and lacking advancement opportunities; these jobs are one form of a secondary labor market. Retention jobs, designed to attract and retain valued skilled employees, represent a minority of part-time jobs in the primary labor market. Tilly does not attribute the primary growth in part-time jobs to demographic shifts, unemployment, or a widening gap between part-time and full-time wages. Rather, he relates the growth to changing employer needs and strategies, including short-time jobs, no benefits, and improved technology that obviates the reliance upon full-time workers.

Many of the characteristics described above are defined by Polivka and Nardone (1989) as contingent work. Rather than blaming the victim (i.e., the part-time worker) for lacking labor force attachment, Polivka and Nardone focus on the terms of employment that characterize contingent work: low degree of job security, including a lack of commitment for future employment; unpredictable variability in hours; and inaccessibility to benefits, especially health insurance. Hence, most, but not all, contingent workers are part of the secondary labor market; those who are not, according to Polivka and Nardone, are voluntary in skilled occupations.

Belous (1989) describes the world moving in the direction of a contingent economy. Unlike a more humane share economy (e.g., a Japanese lifetime employment model) with strong worker affiliation and high flexibility, a contingent economy maintains the same high flexibility with weak worker affiliation. In order to stay internationally competitive, according to Belous, flexibility is necessary. However, in order to accommodate this shift, Belous advocates for a flexible corporate social welfare system, that includes prorated employee benefits, portable pensions, and strong commitment to equal employment opportunity and affirmative action.

The National Association of Working Women, 9 to 5, has also studied the plight of part-time workers. In their September, 1986 report, *Working at the Margins: Part-Time and Temporary Workers in the United States*, part-time working women are described as disempowered. Part-time and temporary jobs, an effective demand-side labor strategy for business cost containment, are reducing the number of full-time jobs and increasing the number of involuntary part-time workers. These workers are poorly paid (57.7 percent of the hourly wage of full timers in 1984), explained in two-thirds of the cases by the high concentration of part-time workers in lower paid retail trade and services industries. Besides, these workers are considered by many employers to have marginal labor force attachment and are, therefore, not worth the investment in training and higher hourly rates of pay.

As part-time and temporary jobs increase, the number of workers with employer-provided health insurance decreases, particularly in non-union companies. Hewitt Research Associates determined in their 1985 survey of 500 non-union companies that less than half of these companies offered health insurance to part-time workers employed 20-29 hours on average per week (*Benefits for Part-Time Employees*, 1985). The Employee Benefits Research Institute (EBRI) estimates that 42 percent of part-time workers have no access to health insurance benefits, either their own or a spouse's group health plan. In their own right (and not through a spouse), part timers with group health insurance coverage amount to only 15.6 percent.

Also according to 9 to 5, the extent of pension coverage is low, creating a grim outlook for adequate living. Because the Employment Retirement Income Security Act (ERISA) does not protect workers with fewer than 1000 working hours per year, many women who work under this prescribed amount are unable to accrue retirement credits. Without pension coverage, female part-time workers are particularly at risk economically in their later years.

Working at the Margins points out how part-time working women are often ineligible for unemployment compensation, since many states require minimum annual earnings. Consequently, significant numbers of women who work less than full time have no economic protection when they lose their jobs. Only 6 out of 50 states permit less-than-full-time applicants to be eligible for unemployment benefits.

Part-time and temporary workers suffer economically both directly and indirectly. Directly, they lose out on pay, pensions, and unemployment compensation. Indirectly, they lose out on job security, advancement, and training programs, all of which amount to money in the long run. They are also less protected than full-time workers by union membership. In 1985, 7.3 percent of part-time workers belonged to labor unions compared to 20.4 percent of full-time workers (BLS, Employment and Earnings, January, 1986).

Whereas Kahne recommends her "New Concept" part-time work as a remedy for the current problems of part-time workers described above, 9 to 5 is more disparaging and pessimistic about part-time work as a solution for women's problems. The surge in temporary and other contingent part-time jobs has worsened the problems for older workers, laid off more frequently for reasons of business necessity. These "disposable employees" (duRivage, 1986, p.6) act as a buffer group against economic uncertainty and allow for the reduction of full-time permanent positions. In addition, these marginal workers have contributed in part to the stagnation of real hourly compensation since the early 1970's (Report of the Joint Economic Committee, 1987, p.13) and to the proportional increase in relatively low-status jobs at the expense of higher status jobs for workers age 35 or older since 1979 (Bluestone and Harrison, 1986).

Hence, 9 to 5's policy recommendations are primarily to convert temporary and part-time jobs, that are increasingly involuntary part-time jobs, into full-time opportunities, including shorter full-time work weeks, (perceived as one solution for some of Germany's unemployment problems). However, this approach, according to 9 to 5, should not be at the expense of voluntary part-time employment with legal protections: equal pay rates; increases in the minimum wage indexed to inflation; universal health insurance; eligibility for all benefits, full or prorated; pension eligibility at 500 rather than 1000 hours per year; family and medical leave without jeopardizing job security; and opportunities for better jobs and promotions.

In a follow-up study to *Working at the Margins*, 9 to 5 addresses the particular vulnerabilities of older workers: *Social Insecurity —The Economic Marginalization of Older Workers* (1987). These older workers are a growing part of the part-time and temporary workforce described in their earlier report. As part of the marginal workforce, they are more likely to work part time rather than full time because full-time jobs are not available. The number of women 45 and older involuntarily working part time has risen from 509,000 in 1979 to 767,000 by 1986 year-end, an increase of over half. From 1965 to 1983 the increase in involuntary part-time schedules for workers between 45 and 65 years of age was 64 percent for men and 108 percent for women. Beyond age 65 this increase amounts to 47.5 percent for men and 97 percent for women (*Handbook of Labor Statistics*, BLS, 1985, Table 21).

With plant closings and company mergers, older workers are prone to layoffs, early retirement, or reemployment at a lower wage. In one study of displaced job losers, this permanent displacement affected 17 percent of men and 22 percent of women 55 and older, bearing in mind that workers 55 plus are only 13 percent of the total labor force (Flaim and Sehgal, 1985). Once laid off, these older workers are less likely to be reemployed. An average layoff for an older worker is one and a half times that of a younger worker: 23.7 versus 15 weeks. Over one-third of displaced workers past 55 never return to the workforce. Past 55, the number of both part-time and full-time women workers drastically decline, whereas the severity of reduction for men is mostly for those in full-time schedules, not part-time (Golden, 1987).

This displacement of older workers has the effect of masking the unemployment problem for older workers. Because of longer periods of unemployment and few, if any, opportunities of reemployment, many become discouraged and drop out of the labor market by retiring. Between 55 and 64 years of age both the mean and median duration of weeks of unemployment in 1986 were highest of any age group: the mean was 23.7 weeks and the median 11.2 weeks (Employment and Earnings, BLS, January 1987). However, at age 65 and beyond, the decline was greatest of any age group: the mean was 16.0 weeks and the median was 6.7 weeks. This probably reflects a dropout from the labor force that is particularly prevalent among older women workers (OWL Report on the Status of Midlife and Older Women, 1986; Rones, 1983; Scott and Brudney, 1987). In addition to job loss, these older workers suffer the additional disadvantages of less education, limited work experience in many declining industries, poorer health, and facing an increasing demand for workers with new technological skills and knowledge of new production methods.

Many older workers who are reemployed suffer significant earnings losses. Older women in both blue and white collar service jobs, particularly those with seniority of 10 years or more, have the largest percent of average earnings losses: 31.2 percent (versus 21.5 percent for men) in blue collar jobs and 30.3 percent (versus 19.8 percent for men) in white collar and service jobs (Podgursky and Swain, 1986, Table 7).

According to the 9 to 5 1987 report, retirement is often the best of bad choices, which might include a prolonged, discouraging search for reemployment; offer of a lesser job in terms of both status and pay; and offer of "involuntary" early retirement in response to a fear of job lay-off. Although early retirement has been on the rise (Crown, et. al., 1987), recent polls have indicated that most older workers would prefer to work, especially part time, rather than retire altogether. Seventy-nine percent of those 55 to 64 and 73 percent of those 65 plus, polled by Louis H. Harris (Sheppard and Montovani, 1982), would have preferred to continue working part time. Comparable findings are noted by the American Association of Retired Persons (Rosen and Jerdee, 1987); here, workers express an interest in postponing retirement if they can work part time, job share, or gradually retire. It should be noted, however, that there is a possibility of response bias from those surveyed; respondents may be giving a socially acceptable answer by stating a continued interest in working part time. Also, studies indicate that perceptions and attitudes about working change quickly after retirement (Morgan, 1980; Goudy, 1981; Schulz, 1988).

The income security of older women is particularly at risk. They are on "shaky legs" (Golden, 1987, p. 65), because the three legs of retirement income (pensions, Social Security, and savings) are weak and unstable for them. Earned income for generating savings is threatened, given the increasing number of job losses and persistent low wages and pay gaps between men and women. Private pension income for older women workers is often deficient; only 20 percent of women, compared to 43 percent of men, receive benefits from their longest held job (OWL Report on the Status of Midlife and Older Women, 1986). In the sales and service sectors, where most women are concentrated, only 27.5 percent of part-time workers receive pension coverage. Because of their limited job tenure and lack of meeting pension vesting requirements, many women have been excluded from eligibility. Those who do qualify are disproportionately in the public sector. The number eligible for pensions is shrinking, especially with the surge in part-time, temporary and contracted-out workers who usually do not qualify for any employee benefits.

Age discrimination also plays a significant part in the employment and reemployment problems of older women, according to a 1980 report of 9 to 5, *Vanished Dreams: Age Discrimination and the Older Worker*. There are several reasons for this phenomenon. First, older women, and older minority women in particular, are more apt than their younger counterparts to be stuck in dead-end, low-paying jobs. Second, the earnings gap between men and women increases with age—e.g., women's wages are 56 percent of a man's wage for those 55 to 64, compared with 76 percent of a man's wage for workers 20 to 24. In addition, women over 40 are three times more likely than men to be unemployed and unemployed longer than younger women (17.7 weeks versus 11.7 weeks), so that they may settle for an involuntary part-time job because they cannot find full-time work. Also, there are many myths about older women workers: they are perceived as less reliable, as more prone to leave or change jobs or to be absent from work, as less mentally and intellectually capable, and as significantly less educated than men or younger women. (In actuality, women ages 54 to 64 complete on average 12.3 years of schooling as compared to 12.1 years for men of the same ages. The median years of schooling for younger women is 12.9, just above the median for older women.) Furthermore, according to *Vanished Dreams*, there are enormous barriers in seeking jobs after age 40, in job mobility, in promotions, and in training/retraining programs. Older women maintain low wages, limited by minimal recognition for years of experience, and salary ceilings in clerical job categories.

QUANTITATIVE STUDIES

The literature on part-time employment focuses mostly on supply-side phenomena—that is, the increase in part-time employees and the changing composition of the labor force. The proliferating numbers in the labor force of married women with children, students helping to finance their education, and elders phasing into retirement, along with the expansion of jobs in the service sector, are all considered factors contributing to part-time employment growth (Kahne, 1985).

The question is: which came first—expanding numbers of workers on the supply side or employer economic concerns leading to the increase in use of less costly part-time workers on the demand side? Like Tilly (1991), Ehrenberg, Rosenberg, and Li (1986) make the argument in their research that demand-side forces are responsible for the surge in total part-time employment. The cost advantages for employers include reduced wages, few or no fringe benefits, and lower degree of union membership. Controlling for cyclical factors (by utilizing unemployment rates for four time trends, 1955-1984, 1963-1984, 1968-1984, and 1973-1984), the researchers analyze the increasing involuntary nature of part-time employment since 1963. Between 1968 and 1984, women have increasingly been found to work part-time involuntarily, whereas men show the reverse pattern. Using data from the March 1984 Current Population Survey (CPS) of approximately 122,000 individuals ages 14 and older, who are employed wage and salary workers working less than 35 hours during a survey week and not self-employed, the researchers estimated how part-time/full-time wage and fringe benefit differentials have varied across industries at one point in time. These estimated differentials, entered as explanatory variables in a simple structural model of the inter-industry determinants of part-time employment, are then used to estimate their effects. The control variables include years of completed schooling, proxies for years of potential employment experience (age minus years of school minus 5) and experience squared, number of children in the family, and dichotomous variables for marital status, gender, race, veteran status, hispanic ethnicity, student status, residence in a standard metropolitan statistical area and in various census regions.

On the demand side of the market, the relative use of part-time more than full-time workers is influenced by relative wage cost differential across industries. This variation explains in part why industries, such as petroleum and coal, with higher costs, employ 2 percent part-time workers and why retail trade, with lower costs, employs 40 percent part time. On the other hand, it is interesting to note that the likelihood of pension coverage, and its effect on the demand (or, more precisely, the lack of demand) for part-time workers does not work in the same direction as wage costs. With regard to pensions, the greater the differential between the probability of pension coverage for full-time and part-time employees in an industry, the smaller (rather than the larger) the relative demand for part-time workers. The explanation given by Ehrenberg, Rosenberg, and Li for this seemingly paradoxical effect is that pension coverage tends to increase workers' predicted tenure with companies and to reduce turnover, which amounts to savings greater than the additional costs of pension coverage for part-time employees. However, *actual* rather than *expected* job tenure data of part-time workers is available in the March 1984 CPS, so that there is a way of testing this hypothesis.

Another explanation for these results might be related to ERISA regulations that require pension coverage of part-time workers employed 1,000 hours per year or more in companies offering coverage to full-time workers. What is missing from this research is any discussion of the relationship between increasing hours of part-time work and pension and health insurance coverage. Also, these negative patterns of estimated differentials (most significantly negative for health insurance and least negative for union membership) are industry-related rather than worker-related, so that important data about individual demographics and economics are excluded from the model.

Schofield (1984) addresses issues of private pension coverage of part-time workers. Schofield draws her analysis from a May 1979 Current Population Survey of Pension Plan Coverage, the first representative data available on part-time workers and their pension coverage. Part-time workers are compared to full-time workers on the basis of labor force characteristics: industry, occupation, size of firm, and union representation. And, for each labor force characteristic three aspects of pension coverage status are reviewed: pension plan availability, non-participation in a plan, and coverage. Although married women comprise over half of the female part-time sample of 8,896 (52 percent), the remaining (nearly half) are single: 36 percent, never-married; 10 percent, widowed and divorced; and 2 percent, married with spouse absent. Of these same women working part time, 16 percent (1,379) are 55 and older, compared to a smaller percentage

(11), but a larger total number of women, working full time (2,297). Because ERISA's cut-off for pension eligibility is 1,000 hours per year, which is approximately equivalent to half time, all those working less than half time are calculated together. Thirty-five percent of white women (8,575) and twenty-seven percent of black women (725) work part-time hours, either more or less than half time. Hence, the profile of the part-time woman is most likely: white; married; and either under 25 years (40 percent), between 30 and 44 years (26 percent), or 55 and older (16 percent).

Only 9 percent of part-time workers are covered by private pensions. The major factor contributing to this low percent is their location in small size companies. In other words, after controlling for the effects of industry, occupation, union membership, and annual earnings, size of firm is the most significant predictor of private pension coverage for ERISA-eligible workers. Part-time workers covered by pensions are more likely to work in large firms of 50 or more employees, yet less than one-fourth of this group actually participate in a plan. Participation in a plan is influenced by ERISA criteria: work tenure of one year or more, minimum age of 21, and 1,000 or more annual hours of work at a pension-covered plan.

Second to size of firm as an important predictor of pension plan coverage is union representation. Part-time workers are three times less likely than full-time workers to have union representation (8 versus 27 percent). Yet, those working part time with union representation are much more likely to have pension plans. Women employed part time are at risk because of both their sex and their employment status. They have lower pension coverage rates, lower participation rates, and lower plan availability rates than women full timers. And, women working full time have lower rates in all three dimensions than men who also work full time. The problem of private pension coverage for women part-time workers is two-fold: lack of plan availability and ERISA ineligibility (that is, not meeting the ERISA criteria, primarily the 1,000 hour per year minimum participation requirement). In both instances, this includes over three-fifths of women part-time workers.

Blank (1990) explores the effect of part-time work on both employee benefits (pensions and health insurance) and wages. Blank draws her data from questions related to workers' employment in 1987 in the March 1988 Current Population Survey (CPS). The sample includes all persons ages 18 through 65, not in school, retired, disabled, or self-employed: 25,143 women (including 17,441 wives and 7,702 single heads of households) and 26,384 men. Clearly, most part-time workers earn lower wages than equally skilled full-time workers in the same industry and region. They also are more likely not to have employee benefits. Also, involuntary part timers receive lower wages and are even less likely to receive employee benefits than equivalent voluntary part-time workers.

Blank uses probit estimates to determine the probability that a worker is included in a pension or health plan. Higher age, higher education, and higher unionization rates contribute to higher probability of receiving a pension for both men and women. Interestingly, the proportion of women in an industry increases the probability of both sexes receiving a pension.

Health insurance coverage is in some ways different for men than for women. The probability of inclusion in a health plan is positively affected by age for men, not for women. And, married women are much less likely of getting health insurance. For both men and women, education levels as well as higher industry unionization rates positively affect health coverage, whereas higher state unemployment rates negatively affect health coverage. Like pension equations, health plan equations show a strong significant negative coefficient on the part-time dummy variable, with even a more significant effect for involuntary part-time workers. Comparing married full-time working women to full-time men, there is a 20 percent probability differential; the former have a 59 percent probability of inclusion in a health plan, compared with 79 percent probability of the latter. In contrast, equivalent women part-time workers have only an 18 percent probability of health coverage, compared with 42 percent for part-time men. Unlike the effect on wages, the effect of part-time work on the receipt of both health and pension plans does not vary across occupations.

From several ordinary-least-squares wage regressions on female and male workers, estimates are drawn of the effects of part-time work on wages. The variables included are all those typically related to human capital (e.g., age, education, marital status, children under 6, and family size) as well as to industry and regions. Blank determines that personal characteristics do not distinguish wages of part timers from those of full timers. Part-time working women in professional, managerial, and technical occupations receive particularly positive repayments. Using the 1987 CPS data, the returns to human capital characteristics for part timers are essentially similar to those of full-time workers. Also, part-time workers do not seem to suffer as much from working in traditional female industries, and they are not strongly affected by regional unemployment rates. And, when all other differences are accounted for, the effect of being involuntarily unemployed is significant and negative.

The effect of part-time work is different for men than for women. Male part-time workers with education and experience equivalent to that of full-time workers are paid less in part-time jobs, even after their choice of working part time is accounted for. However, with women, there is a correlation between their wage rates and their choice to work part time. These differences among women may demonstrate who chooses to work part time as well as what is the nature of these part-time jobs. Part-time working women have different jobs from full-time working women.

When Blank questions if part-time jobs are "bad," the answer is partly determined by the presence of *real* choice to work part time, the data for which is unavailable from the CPS interviews. In other words, many women, who say they work part time voluntarily, may actually prefer to work full time if they could find adequate dependent care.

Unlike Blank who looks at only the availability, not the amount, of pension coverage for most workers throughout the lifespan, Crown, Mutschler and Leavitt (1987) focus their study on older workers 60 years of age and older and the value of their private pension income. They hypothesize that these two factors (i.e., age and pension receipt) are primarily responsible for withdrawing from full-time work prior to age 62. Their sample is derived from Wave 4 of the Survey of Income and Program Participation (SIPP) from the Bureau of the Census. Only 44 percent of people (54 percent men) ages 60 and 61 worked in 1984. This finding indicates that the private pension system serves as a very powerful incentive for retirement, even more so than eligibility for Social Security benefits.

Part-time labor force participation is proportionately more frequent among older women than older men, especially between ages 60 and 65 and then again between ages 70 and 74. Also, single never married older persons are more likely to work more part-time hours than married persons: 8.9 percent versus 6.3 percent. Yet, divorced/separated persons are more than twice as likely to work full time: 16.1 full time versus 7.3 part time. And, widowed persons are least likely to work part time or full time (4.5 and 4.4 percent respectively).

In terms of a racial comparison of those employed, after age 60 blacks are least likely to work part time and Hispanics most likely. Interestingly, Asians are most likely of all races and ethnic groups to work full time (19.9 percent) followed by Hispanics at 12.8 percent, who also have the highest rate of part-time employment. Related to household composition, of the part-time older workforce, over one quarter (26.5 percent) are primary "individuals" living alone, yet most of the remainder (69.7 percent) are married couples ("primary family").

In contrast, of the full-time older workforce 17.7 percent live alone and 80.6 percent live with a spouse.

Part-time workers, according to Crown, et. al.'s 1987 study, are only about half as likely to have attended graduate school: 6.9 percent versus 12.5 percent of full timers. Compared to full-time employees, those working part time are somewhat more likely to work in technical/administrative positions (36.4 versus 29.5 percent) and over two times more likely to be employed in service occupations (33.5 versus 14.2 percent). The industries for which part-time employees work are primarily professional services and retail, and these industries amounts to almost 50 percent of all part-time jobs in all industries.

From tabulations of Wave 4 of SIPP (1984), average monthly earnings for all part-time workers 60 years of age and older were $422.60 with median monthly earnings of only $300. Yet, their average and median total monthly income is over 2 1/2 times as much: $1,075.51 average and $860 median. Although those working full time have much higher monthly earnings ($1,426 and $1,658.55 as the median and average amounts respectively), total monthly incomes reflect a relatively small increase above their earnings: almost $400 average increase and $150 median increase. This is an interesting and important finding which suggests that even though part-time workers earn much less per month than full-time workers and have less income per month, the percent of their non-earnings monthly income is substantially greater than full-time workers. Seventy-six percent of part-time employees receive Social Security, as compared to only 20.7 percent of full-time employees. Part-time workers are more likely to receive other benefits as well, especially union or company pensions (18.3 percent versus only 7.9 percent for full-time workers). However, when comparing men to women, women are less than half as likely to collect pensions (12.3 percent versus 29.3 percent for men). That gap narrows between men and women receiving Social Security to 80.6 percent of women and 75.6 percent of men, although the amount received by women is lesser. Also, women and older elders are more likely to receive SSI and food stamps in addition to Social Security.

Part-time workers rely on the same percentage (37) of their average total monthly income from Social Security as they do from earnings. Only 10 percent of these workers' income comes from pensions. On the other hand, full-time workers rely on 78 percent of their income from earnings, only 8 percent from Social Security, and merely 5 percent from pensions. In contrast to those working both part time and full time, those persons out of the labor force altogether (i.e., retired) receive a much higher percent of their average monthly income from Social Security (57) and from pension benefits (14). Because

Crown, et. al.'s 1987 study documents that much of the earnings loss is regained from other sources, there is little incentive to continue working following retirement. When individuals do so, most choose part-time employment either because they like or financially need to work, not because of poor health or a lack of full-time opportunities.

Crown, Mutschler, Schulz, and Loew (1993) address specifically the economic vulnerability of divorced older women in terms of pensions (both public and private), earnings, assets, divorce benefits (child support and alimony), and public assistance/Supplemental Security Income (SSI). Data sources include four large data sets: the 1990 Current Population Survey (CPS), the 1984 Survey of Income and Program Participation (SIPP, also used in this study), the 1988 Consumer Expenditure Survey (CES), and the National Longitudinal Survey of Older Women (NLS). The sources of income for the "well-off" (i.e., with total incomes of $20,000+) divorced women 62 years of age and older in 1989 are primarily attributed, in descending order, to interest (nearly 90 percent), earnings (63 percent), and Social Security (55 percent). On the other hand, the almost sole source of income for poor divorced women is Social Security (80 percent), with interest (less than 30 percent) and earnings (less than 10 percent) falling far behind as second and third sources (U.S. Bureau of Census, "Current Population Survey" Annual Demographic File, March 1990, p. 23).

Although all four groups of single older women (widows, never married, divorced, and separated) have substantially higher rates of poverty than married older women, the divorced and, even more significantly, the separated women of this age group are most at risk economically. Of course, their economic status varies by age, labor force participation, and measures of economic status (e.g., income, expenditures, and wealth). As anticipated, labor force participation has a strong positive association with economic status. Earnings of working older women contribute significantly to higher incomes. Labor force participation includes those working both full time and part time who represent three racial groups: Whites, Blacks, and Latinos. Divorced Whites are most likely to work full time (23 percent) or part time (14 percent), whereas Blacks and Latinos work least—full time or part time (22 percent altogether for each minority group).

Separated White women are also more likely to work full time (16 percent) or part time (15 percent). Separated minority older women work less full time and part time, putting them most at risk of poverty. The "choice" to separate rather than divorce may be related to two primary factors: inability to afford or access the legal system and cultural biases that preclude divorce.

Private pensions combined with Social Security reduces greatly the risk of poverty among divorced and separated women 62 and over. In fact, only 5 percent of these women are in poverty. However, most divorced and separated women do not receive both private pensions and Social Security. Sixty-five percent receive only Social Security, 3 percent receive only pensions, 10 percent receive neither, and 23 percent receive both.

Kaplan (1985) specifically addresses issues of older working women ages 65 and over. Since 1970, although an increasing number of women of all ages under 65 are staying or returning to the workforce, the labor force participation rate for women over 65 has remained between 8 and 9 percent for the past century. Kaplan uses as her data set the March 1982 Current Population Survey (CPS) of the U.S. Bureau of the Census. Kaplan extracts from the 9,164 retired women 65+ in this survey a 9 percent random sample that is equivalent in size to the 834 (8 percent) women 65+ still working. Both the larger and smaller samples are used for the descriptive statistical part of the analysis in which working women are compared to retired women in order to ascertain how they differ from one another.

Her findings include: (1) working women have more total workers and earners in their households than do retired women—26.4 percent workers versus 20 percent retired; (2) most working women who are married with a spouse present also have a spouse working (over 90 percent), whereas most retired women have spouses not in the workforce (93 percent); (3) female heads of households without a spouse account for over 62 percent of working women as compared to approximately 53 percent for retired women; (4) about 8 percent of families with working women are at or below the poverty level in contrast to almost 21 percent of families with retired women, and income derived from wages and salaries is most significant to the total personal and family income for the working women; (5) the mean income from self employment in families of working women (about 14 percent) is more than twice that received in families of retired women, even though the maximum amounts received by the highest earners are essentially the same, around $60,000; (6) the mean Social Security benefit received by families of working women is 80 percent less than average benefits received by families of retired women, and SSI received by individual working women is, on average, 10 percent of the mean benefit received by retired women; (8) where working women are needy, they appear needier than their retired counterparts, as reflected by a higher maximum benefit for food stamps paid to working women ($2,172 versus $1,996 to retired women) and by a higher maximum payment for energy assistance ($1,000 versus $687 per year for a retired woman); (9) individual retired women, but not their families receive almost three times the average benefit as working women for combined veteran's benefits, unemployment compensation, and worker's compensation—$114 versus $49; and (10) the largest percent of income for families of retired women comes from a combination of Social Security and other government entitlements only (e.g., SSI), whereas those same combinations amount to only 3 percent for families of working women.

In Kaplan's study, 42 percent of retired women give retirement as their primary reason for not working. Thirty-nine percent list taking care of the home and family as the primary reason for not working. Illness and disability are cited as another primary factor (18 percent) for deciding not to work in the year prior to the survey (1981). Compared to their working counterparts, retired women tend to be older with more limited education. Also, they are more likely to be married or widowed.

Of those working, about 61 percent (507) of older women 65+ work part time—i.e., fewer than 35 hours per week. The principal reason for part-time work is choice: they do not wish to work full time. However, 7 percent of those working fewer than 35 hours a week consider themselves full-time workers. Illness is given by only 4 percent as the chief reason for part-time employment, yet none note physical disabilities.

An interesting finding is that although the majority of the sample members work part time, over 60 percent work full year, (data that is often missing in the research on part-time workers). Occupationally, these older women workers are predominantly hourly employees, clerical and service workers, with limited salary income and few private pensions or health plans.

Although Kaplan includes 10 independent variables in her regression equation (pension and health care benefits, industry, health, wage rate, marital status/number of earners, other income, education, age, and race), only pension and health care benefits and industry are statistically significant in relation to hours of work. About 25 percent of the variation in the dependent variable, hours of work, is explained by the existence of a pension plan and the inclusion in a health plan (constructed as one interactive variable since the total number for both is the same). In other words, hours of work increase for older women when they work for a company with a pension plan (although they may not necessarily be vested) and have access to health insurance (yet it may not necessarily be paid for by the employer).

Industry, specifically the industry of the longest job held during the year prior to the survey, is the other significant variable, which accounts for about 13 percent of the variation in weekly hours of work of older women. The variable for industry is split into service producing (e.g., transportation, retail, finance, real estate, and professional services) and non-service producing (e.g., agriculture, construction, and manufacturing). Women in the service sector are more likely to work more hours per week.

REMAINING KNOWLEDGE GAPS

Although there are increasing numbers of research studies that address employment issues facing the elderly, knowledge gaps exist regarding older single women working part time. Many studies of older workers are qualitative and are not based on empirical data. Of the more quantitative research studies, certain variables are often excluded that may skew the findings as they relate to older women part-time workers. For example, independent variables such as regional location, company type (i.e., public or private), and work site size have not been considered in research designs of studies involving older workers and, more specifically, single older women workers. Employee benefits other than pensions are infrequently considered. Even more rare are studies that look at differing hours of part-time work as a dependent variable; rather, most research lumps together all hours of part-time employment between 1 and 34 hours.

Although Schofield's study addresses fully the availability of pensions for part-time workers, her results reflect the overall patterns of pension availability for women part-time workers of all ages, both married and single. Yet, there may be significant differences when only single older women are considered. Some of these women may have longer work histories at one job and, therefore, more likelihood of eligibility for vesting in firms offering pension plans. Also, although Schofield determines that size of firm is the primary predictor of private pension coverage for all ERISA-eligible workers, this may or may not be true when only single older women are considered. Differing hours of part-time work, not analyzed by Schofield, may make a difference in pension eligibility. In other words, closer-to-full-time workers (e.g., 28-34 hour-per-week workers) may be more likely to work in firms that offer pensions and to be vested. Schofield set the stage for analyzing pension availability; now further investigation can be performed using a more limited subcategory of the population of part-time workers. Also, the same questions can be asked and analyzed regarding the availability of another important employee benefit, health insurance.

Unlike Schofield, Blank does analyze the availability of health insurance in addition to pension benefits for both men and women, part timers and full timers. However, she too focuses on all ages of part-time and full-time workers, both married and single, which thereby limits the relevance of her research to single older women 55+. And again, having only one category of part-time work restricts the possibility of determining differences between those who work less than or more than half time.

Although Crown, Mutschler, and Leavitt's study considers age, marital status, race/ethnicity, education, occupation, industry, family type and full-time/part-time work status, these variables may not be sufficient in explaining the extent of part-time work among elders; regional location, company type, and work site size may also influence significantly the number of elders in part-time jobs. Also, this study relates to all workers and to the comparative subgroups of men and women, not specifically to any one subgroup—e.g., older single women. Besides, the working patterns of those 60 and older, the target group of this research, may be quite different from those 55-59. And, part timers in Crown, et al.'s analysis include all those working 1-34 hours per week with no differentiations made according to hours of work per week.

The Crown, et. al.'s 1993 study pays substantial attention to the relationship between sex, age, marital status (i.e., different categories of singlehood), race, earnings, pension, asset holdings, and economic status. Yet, it ignores other demographic and employment factors (such as education, regional location, work site size, company type, and, most importantly for this research study, specific hours of work rather than part time versus full time as the two categories of labor force participation).

Kaplan has analyzed patterns of labor force participation of older women, yet her study is limited to women age 65 and older. Employment patterns between 55 year olds and 65 year olds, especially women, may show even greater significant differences than those between ages 55 and 60 (the age at which Crown, et. al. begin their analysis). Also, Kaplan's research includes a comparison of all women 65+, yet there may be differences in findings when looking at only single women. Thirdly, Kaplan, like Crown, et. al., considers "hours of work" as her broad dependent variable, but at no point in her dissertation does she refer specifically to numbers of working hours. When she refers to increased hours, there is no reference to numbers of hours. As mentioned previously, differing hours of part-time work may be a significant variable.

Kaplan compares working women to retired women. She does not make comparisons within her working subsample. Finally, Kaplan does not take into account the significance of regional location, company type, work site size, and government transfers and entitlements. Certainly, part-time jobs, both in terms of the supply of them and the demand for them, may be influenced by these additional variables.

CONCLUSION

This literature review is both descriptive and empirical. With the recent surge in part-time employment for workers of all ages, a great deal has been written about the plight of these workers: underpaid, devalued, unpromoted, and unprotected. Older workers, particularly older single women, are particularly vulnerable—to unemployment and to poverty. Job opportunities are few and menial for the most part, and most women who continue to work do so out of financial necessity because of little or no ongoing income in retirement from pensions or other assets. It is questionable whether a significant number of single older women choose to work because they like their jobs in the primary labor market—that is, women with more education in white collar jobs.

The studies and reports cited above describe primarily part-time work and older workers. Older working women, when considered, are often compared with men and with retired women. Subcategories of these women ages 55 and older, specifically single women of all kinds (i.e., never married, widowed, separated, and divorced) who work varying hours of part time, have received no special attention in research. It is these subcategories of single women ages 55 and over that this study addresses.

Chapter III

Methodology and Research Design

FOCUS OF STUDY

The population of interest in this research study is single women 55+ with varying degrees of labor force participation—i.e., working less than half time (1-17 hours per week), working more than half time (18-34 hours per week), or working full time (35 or more hours per week). Women are defined as single if they are widowed, separated, divorced, or never married. They represent all ages 55 and older, races, geographic areas of the United States, and educational levels. They live alone or with others. They are employed in a wide range of occupations in both the public and the private sectors. Some single older working women receive health insurance from their jobs or unions, the premiums of which are partially or fully subsidized. Some also have access to employer pensions. They are employed in work sites that vary in size. And, of those who work part time, their labor force participation patterns are either voluntary or involuntary. In addition to earnings or hourly wages from employment, these women may or may not have other economic resources: both interest from personal assets and public and/or private pensions (i.e., non-earned income) as well as household wealth (i.e., the value of total assets minus total debts).

The questions raised by the study relate to economic circumstances of the women described above. Do some profiles of single older working women contribute to financial risk more than other profiles? What are the labor force participation patterns (i.e., full time versus less than or more than half time) of those most at risk, and how do these patterns relate to their demographic, employment, and income characteristics? And, is there a difference between those working less than half time and those working more than half time in terms of such factors as access to company health insurance and a retirement plan, types of occupations in public or private firms, and size of work sites? Are single older women's labor force participation patterns a matter of personal choice (i.e., voluntary), or are these women forced to work more or fewer hours because factors in the labor market (e.g., lack of available full-time jobs) or because of financial need? Also, is age a proxy in some ways for working hours and resulting earnings? If so, are working hours influenced by Social Security regulations, that include income ceilings and benefit penalties if earnings exceed enforced limits? Are single older women who work—part time or full time—different from their non-working counterparts on any demographic, employment, or income measures?

The answers to these questions will address issues that affect the economic vulnerability of single older women: e.g., part-time work, low pay, lack of access to employee benefits, unskilled work, limited education, or living alone. If, in fact, single older women are more at risk for living in poverty, profiles of working single women 55 and older may offer information that can help shape employment policies and practices as well as income maintenance programs responsive to their needs. Chapter 6 discusses the specific policy implications of this study's research findings.

The Survey of Income and Program Participation (SIPP), 1984 (Wave IV), from the Bureau of the Census is used as the data source for this study. (A description of the SIPP data set follows later in this chapter under *Source of Data*.) The unweighted sample sizes (amounting to 395 altogether) are 252 of full-time workers (64 percent of the total sample), 62 of 1-17 hour workers (16 percent of the sample), and 81 of 18-34 hour workers (20 percent of the sample). The size of the non-working sample is 2,166, taken from the same SIPP data set. A diagram of this research design is presented in Figure 3.1 that highlights visually the Correlates of Labor Force Status of Single Women 55+.

The statistical analysis is based upon unweighted data because the computer program used for this analysis, SPSS (Statistical Package for the Social Sciences), has a method of weighting that, in effect, inflates the sample size to population counts. As a result, if the weighted data were utilized, the statistical significance of the findings would be overstated.

Significant differences are tested among the three groups of working women related to the following independent variables: (1) age; (2) marital status; (3) level of education; (4) race; (5) living arrangements (living alone or with others); (6) regional location; (7) types of jobs (occupations); (8) reason for part-time work (voluntary or involuntary); (9) receipt of employee benefits, specifically health

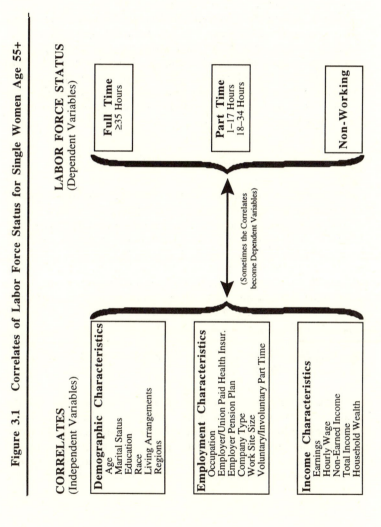

Figure 3.1 Correlates of Labor Force Status for Single Women Age 55+

LABOR FORCE STATUS
(Dependent Variables)

Full Time
≥35 Hours

Part Time
1–17 Hours
18–34 Hours

Non-Working

(Sometimes the Correlates
become Dependent Variables)

CORRELATES
(Independent Variables)

Demographic Characteristics
Age
Marital Status
Education
Race
Living Arrangements
Regions

Employment Characteristics
Occupation
Employer/Union Paid Health Insur.
Employer Pension Plan
Company Type
Work Site Size
Voluntary/Involuntary Part Time

Income Characteristics
Earnings
Hourly Wage
Non-Earned Income
Total Income
Household Wealth

insurance and pensions; (10) company type (private or public); (10) work site size; (11) earnings income; (12) income from non-earnings assets; (13) hourly wage; (14) total income (i.e., earnings plus non-earned income); and (15) household wealth.

Each independent variable will have varying degrees of influence upon the dependent variable, hours of work. Also, it is expected that there may be an interactive effect on hours of work among some of the independent variables. A description of each of the independent variables follows with attention to the specific research hypotheses regarding factors affecting labor force participation and hours of work as well as the interaction of the variable under consideration with other independent variables.

COMPARISON GROUP

Although the primary sample are single older working women, a comparison group has been chosen of non-working single older women from the same data. Again, these data are drawn from the 1984 SIPP (Wave IV). The unweighted sample size of the single non-working women is 2,166, approximately 5 1/2 times the size of the working sample. The purpose of this secondary group is, by comparison, to highlight and to strengthen the findings of this research study. These non-working women are analyzed for similarities and differences according to the same demographic and income variables.

DEFINITIONS AND HYPOTHESES FOR EACH INDEPENDENT VARIABLE

The variable definitions that follow are based upon existing knowledge, a review of the literature, and general understanding of the sample population. The hypotheses about these variables and the interactions between variables are not necessarily supported by specific theory or research. Nevertheless, they still lead to certain questions and expectations of predicted results that are formulated below.

DEMOGRAPHIC VARIABLES

Age

Age here is defined as 55 years of age and older. Age has been recoded into four categories: (1) 55-61; (2) 62-64; (3) 65-69; and (4) 70 and older.

Hypotheses: Age may be a primary determinant of the number of working hours. The "younger" elder single woman ages 55 to 61 may be more likely to work more hours because of enhanced work opportunities, less age discrimination in the workplace, increased energy and improved health status, and fewer demotivators to working, such as penalties on Social Security benefits above the income ceiling between ages 62 and 69. Age, as just suggested, is not the only influence on working hours; it interacts with other variables, perhaps most importantly for the purposes of this research, with receipt of Social Security benefits. There is an anticipated drop in average hours worked among single women ages 62 to 65 correlated with the receipt of early retirement income. The number of hours worked continues to drop progressively for older single working women, ages 66 through 69, which may be correlated with the receipt of full Social Security benefits at age 65 and with the imposition of income ceilings and Social Security penalties on those making more than the allowed amount. Given no imposed penalty after age 70 and, perhaps, greater economic need, (yet more likelihood of declining health and energy with more advanced age), there may be evidence of an increase in hours worked by single women ages 70+.

Marital Status

Marital status includes all single women, defined as widowed, divorced, separated, and never married.

Hypotheses: Widows on average may work fewer hours than other single marital groups because they have less financial need. Because most Social Security benefits available to married women are based upon earnings of husbands which traditionally far exceed earnings of their wives, widows may be more likely to have larger benefits than other single women who are separated, divorced, or never married. Also, their deceased husbands are more likely to have private pensions from their jobs that have been passed on to surviving widows, especially since the inclusion of the mandatory joint survivorship clause with ERISA. There may be a second group of widows who are very poor. Because they receive no or small private pensions and low Social Security benefits, this group may be more apt to work. Never married women may be less economically vulnerable than women of the same age who have been divorced or separated, because they have longer work histories and resulting higher earnings.

Education

Education is defined as years of school completed either at the high school or college level. Education has been recoded into five categories: (1) less than high school completion; (2) high school graduation; (3) some college; (4) college graduation; and (5) beyond college education.

Hypothesis: Older single women with limited education—e.g., with less than a high school diploma—may tend to work fewer hours than those with college education (with resulting enhanced job opportunities and work experiences). Women of this cohort were often not encouraged to pursue education, partly because of the lack of available education and career opportunities as well as a societal de-emphasis on the importance of education for women. On the other hand, these same women with less education may have no choice but to work more hours because their hourly wage or salaries are much less than that of more educated older single women and their economic need, therefore, much greater.

Race

Race is defined here as White and Non-White. Given small sample sizes among minority respondents, Non-White is a recoded variable that includes Blacks, American Indians/Eskimos/or Aleuts, and Asians/Pacific Islanders.

Hypotheses: Women of color are faced with "double jeopardy" in the workplace; they are discriminated against both because of their sex and because of their age. Compounding these barriers to work is their age. It would follow, then, as one hypothesis that single older women of color work less because they cannot find jobs. And, when they do work, they work fewer hours without employee benefits at menial jobs in the secondary labor market—for example, as domestics, sales clerks, and secretaries. Race may serve as a proxy for education: the higher the education, the more likely they are to be White and to work, and the lower the education, the more likely they are to be minorities and not to work. Yet, a contrary theory may be that single older women of color, like those with less education, are forced to work more hours because their salaries or hourly wages are substantially lower and necessitate working for financial survival.

Living Arrangements

Living arrangements refer to the household composition of people, both related and unrelated, living under the same roof. There are two categories of living arrangements: living alone and living with others.

Hypothesis: Single older women living alone, rather than with relatives or other persons, may be more likely to work half time or more part-time hours. Women who have no one with whom to share household expenses are more apt to work more hours.

Regions

Regions refer to four primary areas of the United States: Northeast, Midwest, South, and West. The states are recoded according to the Bureau of Labor Statistics' regional classifications.

Hypotheses: With changing tides in unemployment, regional location may have a significant impact upon the availability of part-time jobs for single older women. A region with low unemployment is more likely to experience strong demand in relation to supply—that is, more job openings than available workers. In response to this economic trend of a tight labor market, there is usually more flexibility of hours offered. As a result, there may be more single older women in part-time jobs who choose to work part time in areas of low unemployment. On the other hand, employers often use part-time workers to reduce labor costs, including reduced benefit costs, without layoffs. Yet, declining regional employment could have the reverse effect of making it more difficult for older persons to get another job if laid off. The degree of part-time work in a region is also influenced by the concentration of job/industry types. Regional industrial mix affects labor force participation and has implications for job opportunities for older workers.

EMPLOYMENT VARIABLES

Occupation

Occupation classifications are based upon the 1980 Census of Population Occupation Classification System. Occupations are recoded into three distinct categories: (1) professional/managerial; (2) technical, sales, service, administrative support; and (3) operators/fabricators. Self employment is excluded as a separate category of employment because the self-employed women in the survey do not have information on their occupations and, therefore, cannot be compared to the other women where occupations are noted. Also, the analysis does not explore occupational longevity—i.e., whether a job is life-long or transitional as a bridge to retirement.

Hypotheses: Because of an imbalance between employment supply and demand related to the nature of a job, single older women may be more likely to hold part-time jobs in expanding occupational categories. For example, with the surge in the service sector and decline in manufacturing, single older women in part-time jobs may be more likely to reflect this employment pattern. Or, as part-time workers, as women, and as older workers (who suffer from "triple jeopardy" related to job discrimination), these women may be overrepresented in the service sector area where wages and earnings are lowest. As with the regional variable, an occupation may reflect the full gamut of part-time hours or have work schedules that cluster around specific numbers of hours.

Reasons for Part-Time Work

The reasons for working part-time are classified as voluntary or involuntary. The subcategories of voluntary part-time employment, recoded from the original data, include: (1) "want to work part time," and (2) "normal hours are less than 35." The recoded involuntary variable consists of: (1) "health condition or disability," (2) "could not find a full-time job," and (3) "slack work or material shortage." A very small percent (3.8%) is not included in either of the above two categories; they represent write-in responses to "other" on the survey instrument. Because these responses are very individual and few, they are not captured in the data.

Hypotheses: The "older" single working women (over age 61) may be more likely to work part time voluntarily because of several factors: less financial need with the onset of retirement monies (public and private), the severe financial penalty on Social Security benefits ($.50 on every $1 in 1984) for working above the income ceiling ($5,160 in 1984), and less physical energy or poorer health. Yet, does it necessarily hold true that "younger" older women are more likely to work part time involuntarily? Perhaps, their job type, educational level, marital status, and earnings also have bearing upon the voluntary/involuntary nature of their part-time employment. For example, women with better jobs, more education, widowed (with additional assets from deceased spouses), and higher earnings may be more likely to choose to work part time.

Employee Benefits: Health Insurance and Pensions

The "fringe" employee benefits most important to workers are health insurance and pensions. Health insurance in this study is defined as a benefit both covered by and partially or totally paid for by employers or unions. Pensions here are defined as a benefit provided for by employers. Yet, the actual amount and conditions (e.g., vesting requirements for eligibility) of the pension are not discussed in this research study.

Hypotheses: First, health insurance and pension coverage are particularly important employee benefits for single older women, who are increasingly vulnerable to sickness, disability, and poverty because of no second income available to them. As single women, they have none of these benefits available to them through a spouse. Since ERISA mandates by law the availability of private pensions to employees working 1,000 hours or more per year (at least half time) in businesses offering pensions to full-time workers, single women who work half time or more per week may be more likely to accrue pensions than part-time workers with less labor force participation. This ruling may also be a reason that part-time workers tend to be employed all year. An alternative hypothesis might be that these women are without pensions because they work in businesses that do not offer pensions as an employee benefit, totally unrelated to their hours of work.

Access to a group health insurance plan from an employer as well as partial or total payment of insurance premiums are strong incentives to keep working. Many elders are ineligible for individual health plans and/or cannot afford to pay the premiums on their own. Although President Clinton has proposed universal health insurance that would provide eligibility to most workers (both full and part-time), there is presently no federal law like ERISA that mandates health insurance coverage given a minimum number of work hours per year. Since health insurance is usually not offered to workers employed less than half time, single older women working more than half time may be more apt to receive health insurance coverage. In other words, there may be a significant difference in the number of work hours as they relate to both access to and partial or total payment of health insurance.

Comparing health insurance to pension coverage, older single women may be more likely to receive one more than the other, and this may vary according to the number of hours worked as well as according to their occupation. ERISA regulates pension availability, but there is no comparable federal law regarding access to employee health insurance. Therefore, single women 55+ may be more likely to have pensions than health insurance. Or, those who have pensions may also be more apt to have health insurance.

Company Type

Company type describes whether the sample member's employer is private or public. Self employment, a third category of this variable in the original survey, is excluded because there is no information on occupations for this subcategory which would skew the findings when compared to sample members in the public or private sector.

Hypotheses: A private company, more than a government agency, may have more flexibility in setting employment policies and practices, including the work hours of employees. As such, they may be more responsive to caregiving responsibilities of employees—either with young children or with aging parents—that necessitates working part time. Government agencies are more likely to be under scrutiny from the public and, thereby, may have greater pressure to abide by employment laws, such as the Equal Employment Opportunity Act that protects specific classes of workers, including women and older workers (defined as over 40 years old). It may follow, therefore, that there are more older women working in public agencies and, of these numbers, more working part time.

Work Site Size

The size of a work site relates to the number of workers in a particular facility of a company. A small size is less than 25 employees, a medium size is between 25 and 99, and a large size is 100 to 499. Hypotheses: The size of a work site, along with the type of job, may influence the use of part-time workers. Larger company sites may be more likely to utilize single older women as part-time employees, because larger sites can adapt more easily to a wider range of work schedules. An opposing argument, however, is that larger settings have more administrative bureaucracy that could hinder the use of alternative work schedules. It may follow that companies of a certain size making use of more part-time older women employ these women for an extended number of part-time hours. Or, a contrary hypothesis is that these companies hire more women for fewer hours (thereby providing fewer/no employee benefits, lower wages, and essentially less of a permanent commitment to their part-time employees). In other words, work site size may affect positively or negatively the demand side of part-time labor.

INCOME VARIABLES

Wages and Earnings

There are two different variables used for pay. The first is earnings, recoded as annual earnings (multiplying by twelve) from the monthly data. The second is an hourly wage determined mathematically by dividing annual earnings by the number of hours worked per year.

Hypotheses: It is assumed that single older women have more earnings if they work more hours. In addition to hours of work, intuitively one could argue that type of job (occupation), education, and age are strongly associated with earnings. That is, professionals and managers with higher education and lower ages (i.e., 55-61) are more likely to have higher annual earnings. Race, one could assume, works in the direction of higher earnings for Whites and lower wages for minorities.

If one were to speculate that older single women working more hours have more economic need, then one might hypothesize that widows with assets from their deceased spouses work less and, therefore, earn less. Divorced, separated, or never married women may have more need to work and, therefore, work more hours with resulting higher earnings. Also, those women who share living arrangements rather than living alone and who have non-earned income are less likely to work more hours.

In addition to earnings, hourly wage represents another measure of "economic return to working." Earnings have an accounting relationship with hours and wages, so that earnings are computed by multiplying hours with wages. Wages, unlike earnings, do not necessarily change according to differing hours of work. If they do differ, the reasons are theoretical and behavioral, not accounting. One would assume that in the same way that more working hours are associated with more earnings in a straight linear direction, wages, too, might be on an uphill curve based on working hours, especially part-time hours. In real terms, wages would increase as hours of work increased. On the other hand, women making very high wages may choose to trade off some additional income for more leisure time by reducing the number of hours worked.

Non-Earned Income

Non-earned income is defined here as interest/ income from bank accounts, stock dividends, Social Security, and public/private pensions. It is computed by subtracting total earnings, including self employment earnings, from total income.

Hypotheses: Among single older working women, who have the largest and smallest amounts of non-earned income? It would seem most likely that among these single women widows would have the largest based upon inherited income, both survivor pensions and income producing assets from their deceased spouses. Also, if the dual labor market has afforded better jobs and more opportunity to save for retirement and collect pensions to White, educated women, then it would ordinarily follow that their non-earned—as well as their earnings—income would be higher. Furthermore, one might assume that these women are "younger" because they are more apt to work full time in better jobs that afford them more opportunities to save and amass asset income.

If older single women work full time primarily based upon financial need, it would then make sense that those who work part time have more non-earned income on which to live. On the other hand, so as to not penalize their Social Security benefits (part of their non-earned income), these women might choose to work part time even though their non-earned income may be small, comprised solely of their meager Social Security income.

Total Income

Total annual income is computed by adding total monthly earnings to total monthly non-earned income and multiplying by twelve for an annual aggregate amount.

Hypotheses: If total income represents the cumulative annual finances of what single older working women both earn and amass through savings, investments, public and private pensions, and other sources, then it would follow that all of the demographic factors that are associated with higher earnings and non-earnings would all together affect the total income level. For example, if "younger," White, educated, professional women tend to have higher earnings and non-earned income, obviously the end result is more total income.

Similarly, women working full time are more likely to have higher total income. Earnings represent the largest percentage of their income sources. However, although unlikely, if women work less because they have a substantial amount of non-earned income, then part-time workers may have larger total incomes.

Household Wealth

Total net worth—or household wealth—is defined as total household assets minus total debts. It is a lifetime measure representing the excess of income over expenditures. Home ownership for most older people is by far their largest asset.

Hypotheses: If earnings are often used to amass wealth, then it seems likely that there would be a positive association between earnings and wealth. And, if earnings are a proxy for education, race, and occupation, (factors contributing to the secondary labor market), then these variables also would be associated with earnings.

Hours of work, unless they represent a lifelong pattern, would probably not be related to wealth. Hours of work is variable over the life cycle, particularly for women who have raised children, including the divorced, separated, and widowed women from this research sample.

SOURCE OF DATA

The Survey of Income and Program Participation (SIPP), conducted by the Bureau of the Census, is the data source for this research. The data has been drawn cross sectionally from a nationally representative sample of noninstitutionalized civilians ages 15 and older. Although SIPP has the capacity to compare responses at different points in time, this research study analyzes a sample (panel) of four rotations between September and December 1984 (Wave 4). Respondents have been asked a wide range of questions about income from different sources, including public and private monies as well as noncash government subsidized benefits, earnings, and asset holdings. In addition, they have been asked a broad spectrum of questions about demographic and employment characteristics. All these questions refer to the four months prior to their survey interviews.

During Wave 4 the one month of overlap in which information from all four rotations is included is August 1984. So as to keep the data reliable and consistent, August is used for most of the data analysis in this study. Figure 3.2 shows the rotation sequence for Wave 4 that covers both interview months and reference months. One rotation group is interviewed each month, comprised of approximately one-fourth of the total panel number of 21,000 householders in the 1984 sample. (Four months later this same rotation is interviewed again.) This overlapping design allows for a much larger sample size from which more accurate cross-sectional estimates can be made.

*Figure 3.2 Wave 4: Survey of Income and Program
Participation (1984)*

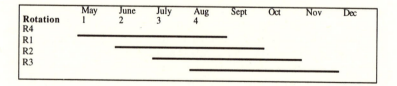

_____Reference Months = 4 Months Prior to Interview Month
Sept - Dec   = Interview Months
Aug   = Only Reference Month with Overlap from All 4 Rotations

Wave 4 is particularly useful because of its topical module (addendum survey) that offers in-depth information about assets, liabilities, pension plan coverage, and prior work characteristics. (Housing characteristics and prior work histories are also major portions of this module, but not included in this study.) Given the depth and breadth of income, earnings, and assets information, SIPP data is considered more relevant and inclusive than any other data set for the purpose of studying the demographic, economic status, and labor force participation of single women 55+ working both full time and part time.

DATA ANALYSIS

This study looks primarily at the individual—the single woman 55 years of age and older—as the unit of measure. Wealth is the only household variable used, which, for most of the sample except for the widows, relates to the individual respondent. SIPP assigns weights to each sample person in order to assure that the estimates of numbers of persons agree with independent estimates of the population within specified age, race, and sex categories.

However, the statistical analysis itself is based upon unweighted data because SPSS (Statistical Package for the Social Sciences), the computer program used for this research, utilized a method of weighting that, in effect, inflates the sample. If the findings were weighted, they would exaggerate the statistical significance of associations.

The analysis begins with looking at the relationships and frequencies of all independent variables with the one dependent variable, hours of work. So that hours of work can be analyzed more carefully, a dependent variable has been created from the data: single women 55+ working less than half time (1-17 hours), working half time or more (18-34 hours), and working full time (35 hours or more).

There could have been many different ways of tabulating the data. Because of the limited sample size, labor force participation was chosen as the dependent variable of central interest. Had it been possible to split the sample not only by hours of work but also by age, for example, policy implications would have been easier to assess; the extent of labor force participation for single older women under 62 and over 62 could have been compared more carefully in order to determine the impact of Social Security on working. As is, the research tries to address issues by looking at such factors as age and marital status within each category of working hours.

Frequencies alone offer a descriptive view of the composition of older single woman in the part-time labor force. These descriptive statistics also provide distributional information, variation, and central tendency data for each variable. In addition to the mean, the median is used to examine total income as a more reliable measure of economic circumstances of single older women. The mean, taking into account outliers, is often skewed by the experience of extreme values in the sample and thereby misrepresents central tendencies in the data.

Statistical measures of association are particularly important to this research analysis. By using crosstabs and chi-square tests, the strength of associations is examined between the dependent variable, hours of work, and each of the independent variables described earlier.

All interval independent variables determined as significant through chi-square tests (plus education considered relevant in the equation, although not significant) have been recoded as categorical and included in two-way analyses of variance (ANOVAs). Several dependent variables are analyzed in the ANOVAs: hours of work, total annual earnings, total annual non-earned income of the working women and total annual income of both the working and non-working women. The dependent variables are all measured on an interval scale. ANOVA looks at differences between the means of different groups, relative to the variation within each group, to assess whether the independent variables explain a significant amount of the variation in the dependent interval variable.

Two-way ANOVAs allow for interactions among the explanatory variables. Each ANOVA has three primary purposes: (1) it disaggregates the portion of variation due to each one of the interval variables; (2) it provides the statistical difference in mean hours worked between different categorical independent variables (e.g., age and marital status); and (3) it automatically looks for the interaction between categories along with main effects. For example, age and access to and payment of health insurance are disaggregated, controlling for household wealth, to determine the source of variance on hours of work. Do mean hours of work differ by age category and/or access to and/or payment of health insurance?

Analysis of variance is not as powerful a statistical method as regression, because it provides information only about statistical significance without imposing directional causality. However, because of the possibility of two-way causality between hours of work and many of the independent variables, such as provision of pensions and health insurance, a regression analysis might offer erroneous findings.

CONCLUSION

For some older women, the decision to work part time or full time is a matter of choice that has nothing to do with economics, demographics, or labor force characteristics. However, for most women, economic resources as well as demographic and employment profiles do play major roles in the decision to work part time or full time in later years. Therefore, measuring the determinants of working differing part-time hours among single older women as they compare to working full time—and not working at all—is important for establishing and reforming employment policy as well as income maintenance policy for this population. The hypotheses tested in this research will address questions related to the income needs of single older women and the degree to which economic need is a factor in the number of hours worked. With a fuller understanding of single older women, who are on average most prone to poverty in old age, both employment incentives and income programs can be designed to better meet their needs and those of society.

Chapter IV

Demographic and Employment Findings

KEY FINDINGS: EFFECTS OF DEMOGRAPHICS, EMPLOYMENT AND INCOME

This research explores the labor force participation patterns of single older women, defined as 55 years of age and older who are single through widowhood, divorce, separation, or never being married. They represent a wide range of demographic, employment, and income characteristics, described and analyzed in Chapters 4 and 5. Their labor force participation patterns, specifically the hours that they work—whether less than half time, more than half time, or full time—are clearly associated with their economic need to work. To further highlight their financial incentive to work, these women are compared to non-working single older women from the same data set according to the same demographic and income variables.

When compared to non-working, the data demonstrate that working makes the most economic difference at the lowest end of household total net worth, yet continues to compare favorably to non-working until the highest level of the wealth category. In each income category, monthly and annual income among single older working women accounts for at least twice that of the non-working women. And, non-working women's monthly income in 1984 is only $47 over the 1983 poverty line. One may infer from this analysis that the strongest motivation to work relates to income. Yet, the similarities among workers and non-workers in the middle two ranges of household total net worth suggests that the motivation to work—or not to work—may have derivations other than money (e.g., job satisfaction, social supports, and caregiving responsibilities) that the data set is unable to test.

As expected, the majority of single older working women stay in the workforce—and even return to it—because they are forced to for financial reasons. Research clearly indicates that most men retire when they are economically able to do so, which for many is at age 62 when they are eligible for early retirement. Single women, on the other hand, who have limited non-earned income, minimal Social Security benefits (under $5,000 a year for all working women in this study) based on low paying jobs, no or small private pensions, and little accumulated wealth, may not have as much option of retiring early.

A surprising proportion (12 percent) of single women work at age 70 and older, almost the same percent who work between ages 62 and 64 (13 percent). Compared to older working women under 70 years of age, the oldest women tend to make the lowest wage and the lowest annual earnings income, whereas their non-earned income is clustered in the two higher ranges. Demographically, the oldest working women are most likely to be widowed and living alone. However, compared to their non-working counterparts, they have on average more education.

Not only are these single older women remaining in the workforce, but the majority in each category are working full time. The proportion range from a low of 55 percent of widows to a high of 79 percent of divorced women, the latter of whom are primarily 55 to 61 years of age and, therefore, ineligible for Social Security. It is also astounding that one quarter of those working beyond age 70 are employed full time and another 29 percent are working more than half time. According to the research findings, single older women working full time on average rely almost exclusively on their earnings, having minimal non-earned income or wealth, although the strength of the findings is limited by the sample size.

One possible reason that single women beyond age 70 do not drop out of the labor force, when they would be most expected to do so for health reasons and preference of leisure over labor, is related to financial need. They are no longer penalized for earnings above the very meager income ceiling ($5,160 in 1984) and are thereby able to keep twice as much of their Social Security benefits. Trying to disentangle the reasons that these women stay in the labor force after age 70 is difficult. They cannot be compared to married women or married men, because their decisions are strongly influenced by the labor force participation of spouses. And, comparing single older women to single men of the same age group is also unrelated, since men in general are able to make retirement decisions more easily, based on economic security from longer and stronger work histories inclusive of more earnings, pensions, and savings.

Whereas, in general, economic need drives single older women to work, the number of hours they work corresponds to their age: the younger their age, the more likely they are to work more hours. This finding seems intuitively obvious, related to both demand and supply labor market factors: on the supply side, younger workers have better health, more energy, minimal amounts of public or private pension benefits, and increased interest in work over leisure; on the demand side, they are better educated, suffer less from age discrimination, and are perceived to have greater work longevity. In addition to age, marital status is strongly associated with working hours. Although widows are the largest subgroup in all three categories of working hours, widows are least represented in the full-time workforce, and divorcees are most represented.

More employment than demographic characteristics are significantly related to working hours. Pink collar workers, comprising two-thirds of the sample, account for most part-time jobs, whereas most white and blue collar workers, although small in numbers, are primarily full time. The data provides further evidence of a contingent, marginal, secondary labor force of part-time single older women who choose to work, (even if fewer hours than desired, at unskilled, low paying jobs), as the lesser of two evils: economic survival rather than abject poverty.

An interesting finding from the data analysis is the strong association between hours of work and both employer/union paid health insurance and employer pensions. Eighty to 88 percent of full-time workers receive total or partial payment of their health insurance from their employers or unions; the percentages represent 18 to 26 points above the overall percentage of full timers in the total sample. In contrast, less than one quarter of the part-time workforce on average can count on their insurance partially or totally paid for through work. Although older people are particularly frightened about their health and the costs of health care, health insurance coverage is increasingly difficult to obtain.

Full-time employment, as demonstrated by the research findings, offers the ticket to both insurance coverage and premium payments, but not to private pension benefits at retirement. As working hours increase among single older women, the percentage of those with retirement plans decreases. As a result, when single older women worry about their health and their financial security at retirement, the future looks grim for many of these women unless they are able to continue working full time or have sufficient non-earned income.

Not only are part-time workers (both less than and more than half-time workers) less likely to receive health insurance at work, but they also tend to be older, widowed, pink collar employees in private, small companies (with under 25 workers). One way of interpreting these findings is that the labor force maintains flexibility of working hours, particularly responsive to those who voluntarily want opportunities working less than full time. However, this interpretation does not address those who are working part time involuntarily:

primarily 55-61 year olds, divorced women, pink and blue collar workers in large private work sites (with 100+ employees).

In comparing the two categories of part-time workers, (less than half time and more than half-time workers), the most noteworthy finding is the substantially lower wage among the more than half-time workers: 18-34 hour per week workers make 71 cents less than the less than half-time workers and $3.11 less than the full timers. And, the total incomes of these 18-34 hour workers is only 9 percent more than that of the 1-17 hour workers. It is unclear why those working more part-time hours make less per hour, and one can only speculate that it is related to a different occupational mix in each category or motivations for working unrelated to earnings, (e.g., access to employee benefits, job satisfaction, or social supports).

PRIMARY SAMPLE

The primary sample is comprised of 395 single working older women, 55 years of age and older who are either widowed, divorced, separated, or never married. An additional 25 percent of working women in this age range and marital status are deleted from the sample because they have 0 hours of work and no earnings, are self-employed with no noted occupation, and/or have no noted earnings income; the inclusion of these women would skew the findings given that the intent of the research is to demonstrate economic vulnerability that is partly determined by the degree of labor force participation (i.e., hours of work), by types of employment, and by amount of earnings income. Sixty-four percent of the sample work full time, 16 percent work less than half time (1 to 17 hours per week), and 20 percent work more than half time (18 to 34 hours per week). The calculations reported in this chapter are unweighted, derived directly from the sample. The independent variables are comprised of three types: demographics, employment characteristics, and income. The demographic variables include age, marital status, education, race, living arrangements, and regions. The employment-related variables include occupation, employer or union paid health insurance, employer provided pension plan, company type (private or public), work site size, and reasons for part-time work (voluntary or involuntary). The income variables include hourly wage, total earnings, total non-earned income which takes into account the amount of pension and Social Security income and income from other sources (rent, asset income, etc.), total income, and household wealth (primarily from home ownership). Because of the small sample size, some of the individual percentages in the tables may be unreliable and should be interpreted with caution. The sample sizes used to calculate the percentages are reported in the tables to enable the reader to assess the reliability.

COMPARISON GROUP

In order to highlight the findings of this research, non-working single older women from the same data set are used later in this chapter and the following chapter as a source of comparison regarding the same demographic and income related variables of this study. The number of non-working women is 2,166, almost 5 1/2 times larger than the size of the working sample. If demographically similar women from the working and non-working samples differ on economic grounds, specifically non-earnings and total income, what part do earnings play in working women's motivation (even desperation) to work while other women from their cohort and age bracket are able to make use of their leisure?

DEMOGRAPHIC VARIABLES

The demographic variables from the SIPP data set that seem to have most relevance to the economic vulnerability of single older working women are those related to age, marital status, education, race, living arrangements, and regions. It is these variables that have been chosen for quantitative description and for statistical analysis.

Age

Age is divided into four categories: 55-61, 62-64, 65-69, and 70+. The rationale for these categories is that they represent important age ranges that correspond in part to government (and private employment) regulations regarding ages for early (62-64) and regular retirement (65+) and resulting eligibility for Social Security benefits. Because of the existence of stringent income ceilings with Social Security eligibility ($5,160 in 1984) and substantial benefit penalties for exceeding the income ceilings ($.50 for every $1.00 earned in benefits in 1984), it is hypothesized that age and the degree of labor force participation, specifically hours worked per week, would be highly correlated. Again, although the data do not ask about the motivations for working part or full time, the percentages of women working in each age range might give some indication about employment motivators or demotivators, such as Social Security benefit ceilings and penalties.

As expected, the largest percent of those working in this sample are the younger single women between 55 and 61 years of age: 60 percent (Table 4.1). The remaining percent working in the next three age categories (62-64, 65-69, and 70+) are distributed relatively equally at 13, 15, and 12 percent of the total. Almost three-quarters of those working full time also fall within this younger age category, as do 46 percent of the group in the 18-34 hour category. These "younger" women working full time comprise by far the largest percent of single working women in all four age categories.

As illustrated in Table 4.1, the 65-69 year olds and the 70+ year olds each represent approximately one-third (34 and 37 percent respectively) of women working less than half time. Although the two older groups of single women are most represented in the part-time categories, primarily working less than half time, their overall percent is essentially no different from that of the 62-64 year olds who, we might assume, are generally more physically and mentally able to work were it not for the restrictions and penalties associated with early retirement.

In analyzing the distribution of hours worked by age (Table 4.2), it is interesting to note the degree of labor force participation among the oldest group; one quarter of single women 70+ who are employed full time, and even more (29 percent) work more than half time. In other words, while they comprise only 12 percent of the overall sample (only one percent less than the 62-64 year olds and only 3 percent less than the 65-69 year olds), they continue to demonstrate a strong labor force attachment. Thirty-two percent of the 65-69 year olds work either more than half time or full time.

Table 4.1 Percent Distribution of Demographic Characteristics by Hours Worked[a]

Sample Size: 395	(n=63)	(n=79)	(n=253)	(n=395)
	Hours Worked			
	1 - 17	18 - 34	> 35	All
Age***				
55-61	18	46	74	59
62-64	11	12	14	13
65-69	34	23	8	15
≥ 70	37	19	5	12
Marital Status***				
Widowed	66	59	44	50
Divorced	15	19	36	29
Separated	5	5	6	6
Never Married	15	17	15	15
Education				
Some High School	45	36	31	34
High School Graduate	37	48	40	42
Some College	13	11	15	14
College Graduate	2	1	8	5
Post-College	3	4	6	5
Race				
White	85	91	84	86
Non-White	15	9	16	15
Living Arrangements				
Living Alone	65	62	53	57
Living with Others	35	38	47	43
Regions				
Northeast	23	25	28	27
Midwest	24	29	23	24
South	39	28	33	33
West	15	19	16	16

Source: Author's Tabulation of U.S. Bureau of the Census, Survey of Income and Program Participation (SIPP), Wave IV, 1984.

[a] Percentages may not add up to 100 due to rounding.
***$p < .01$

Table 4.2 Percent Distribution of Hours Worked by Demographic Characteristics[a]

Sample Size: 395

	Hours Worked			
	1-17	18-34	> 35	All (n)
Age*				
55-61	5	16	79	100 (234)
62-64	13	19	67	100 (51)
65-69	36	32	32	100 (59)
≥ 70	45	29	25	100 (51)
Marital Status*				
Widowed	20	24	55	100 (199)
Divorced	8	13	79	100 (114)
Separated	14	18	68	100 (22)
Never Married	15	23	62	100 (60)
Education				
Some High School	21	21	58	100 (136)
High School Graduate	41	24	62	100 (164)
Some College	15	17	69	100 (54)
College Graduate	5	5	90	100 (20)
Post-College	10	14	76	100 (21)
Race				
White	16	22	63	100 (339)
Non-White	17	13	70	100 (56)
Living Arrangements				
Living Alone	18	22	60	100 (224)
Living with Others	13	18	69	100 (171)
Regions				
Northeast	13	19	68	100 (105)
Midwest	16	24	60	100 (95)
South	19	17	64	100 (129)
West	14	23	63	100 (64)

Source: Author's Tabulation of U.S. Bureau of the Census, Survey of Income and Program Participation (SIPP), Wave IV, 1984.

[a]Percentages may not add up to 100 due to rounding.
***p<.01

The full-time workers are significantly overrepresented (79 percent and 67 percent respectively) in the two youngest age categories (55-61 and 62-64), compared to their overall representation in the total sample (Table 4.2). It is noteworthy that although the percent decline (46 percent) of single working women between the first and second age categories is drastic, 67 percent of those continuing to work between ages 62 and 64 work full time.

There is high statistical significance (p <.01) between age and hours of work. The data on age suggest that age is a proxy for other factors and raise important questions. Besides increasing age, what are some of the other influences on the huge labor force decline at 62? Are they related to availability of early retirement and/or to the steep penalty placed on Social Security benefits (50 percent on every Social Security dollar earned in 1984) beyond the low income ceiling set by the Social Security Administration ($5,160 in 1984)? According to the data, there is strong statistical significance (p <.01) between age and receipt of Social Security benefits (Table 4.3). Of the 29 percent (115 women) receiving Social Security benefits from the entire sample, only 6 percent collect Social Security between ages 55 and 61; this very small percent is equivalent to less than 1 percent of the entire sample. Between ages 62 and 64, when elders are eligible for early retirement benefits, only 8 percent of the entire sample (29 percent of those collecting Social Security) receive benefits. Between ages 65 and 69, when regular Social Security benefits are available, only 22 percent of the total sample (76 percent of those receiving Social Security) receive benefits. However, even after age 70, when the income ceiling and penalty no longer exist, only 27 percent collect benefits (94 percent of those receiving Social Security). These low overall percentages reflect the younger ages in the sample. However, it is important to remember that only 29 percent of the entire sample (115 out of 395) rely on any Social Security as part of their total annual income.

*Table 4.3 Percent Distribution of Social Security by Age****

Sample Size: 115

	Social Security		
	No Benefits	Benefits	Total (115)
Age***			
55-61	97	3	100 (7)
62-64	71	29	100 (15)
65-69	24	76	100 (45)
≥ 70	6	94	100 (48)

Source: Author's Tabulation of U.S. Bureau of the Census, Survey of Income and
Program Participation (SIPP), Wave IV, 1984.
***p<.01

Also, why do these single women beyond age 70 appear to be as likely to work as somewhat younger women (62 and older)? One might assume that these oldest working women may be, on average, least physically able or interested in continuing to work (especially during an age cohort where women have relatively limited education and occupational opportunities)? Because the overall population of older people shrinks with advancing age, the fact that there are the same number of older single women in the workforce at both ages 62-64 and 70+ must be related to more than an artifact of the population age group sizes. Is this phenomenon related to acute financial need of single older women? A demographic comparison by age of these women to non-working single older women, later in this chapter, provides one answer. Issues of economic resources of this working sample compared to those of non-working women offers another answer in the next chapter.

Marital Status

Although all the women in the sample are single, they are single for different reasons—either widowed, divorced, separated, or never married. The separated women, although few in number, have been identified in a distinct category because they often face different issues than divorced women and tend to be more economically vulnerable (Crown, Mutschler, Schulz, Loew, 1993; Loew, 1992).

The data suggest that there is great variation among the different marital status categories of single women, with high statistical significance (p <.01) between hours worked and marital status. Widows of all ages number half of the sample (Table 4.1), followed by the divorced who comprise under one-third (29 percent), with never married women at 15 percent and separated women at only 6 percent. Comparing all single categories of working older women, widows make up an even larger percentage of those working part time: 66 percent work less than half time and 59 percent work more than half time. On the other hand, in the full time category, widows are a smaller percentage (44 percent) than in either part-time category or in the sample of widows altogether.

The reverse is true in the divorced category. Although this subgroup makes up 29 percent of the entire sample, it comprises 36 percent of the full-time workers. Out of necessity, divorced women disproportionately must work full time; they also tend to be younger. In each of the two part-time categories, the divorced are less than one-fifth: 15 percent in the 1-17 hour group and 19 percent in the 18-34 hour group. Compared to never married women, divorced women are almost twice as likely to work.

Based upon the percentage distribution of hours worked by marital status (Table 4.2), in all single marital status categories the largest percent work full time: the proportion in the divorced group is substantially highest at 79 percent, and among the widows, lowest at 55 percent. Also, in all four categories, the smallest percentages work less than half time: 20 percent of widows, 8 percent of divorced, 14 percent of separated, and 15 percent of never married. In other words, although widows represent the largest subgroup of single older women, they represent the smallest percent of those working full time. The divorced, separated, and never married, given their total number relative to the whole sample, are overrepresented in the full time category. Widows represent the largest percentage of those working part time: 44 percent altogether compared to 21 percent of the divorced, 32 percent of the separated, and 38 percent of the never married.

Education

The education variable describes five categories of women: (1) some high school education, (2) graduation from high school, (3) some college, (4) graduation from college, and (5) post-college education (Table 4.1). Over three-quarters of the total sample have only a high school education or less. The largest percent of these work part time: 84 percent at 18-34 hours and 82 percent at 1-17 hours. Those women who attended or graduated from college comprise approximately one-quarter of the total sample, with the smallest percentage who have at least a college degree (10 percent). Among those working full time, only 5 percent more (29 percent) are college educated single women.

Given the relatively limited education of women from this cohort, it is interesting to note the substantial percent of college educated women who remain in the work force. And, of these women, at least 69 percent (with some college) and as much as 90 percent (college graduates) work full time, 7 to 11 percent higher respectively than full-time workers with only high school education, completed or not (Table 4.2). This finding is supported by other recent research that correlates full-time work with college graduate women (Spalter-Roth and Hartmann, 1992).

It could be theorized that working hours might be associated with education positively or negatively. A theory about a positive relationship might be that increased education contributes to better job opportunities with better pay that results in more incentive to work full time. Because earnings are highly associated with single older women's standard of living, these women—as long as they are mentally and physically able to work—may make the choice of labor force participation over leisure.

On the other hand, a theory about a negative association might be that better pay with higher education and quality jobs leads to less financial need to work as single women get older. This hypothesis would suggest that their pay has been substantial enough to allow for amassed savings for retirement, which may contribute to single older women's working only part time, especially less than half time. However, as plausible as these theories are, overall the data suggests that there is no statistical significance between education and hours worked.

Do these women stay in the labor force because of greater job opportunities and higher salaries that are related to their educational level, or are the motivations less tangible, such as job satisfaction? There is no question in the SIPP survey that asks for the reasons that women work full time; it is assumed that full-time work is the standard (or "default") for women, as it is for men, and that "only part-time work" indicates special circumstances. However, from analyzing the data, specifically the relationship between education and both occupation and earnings, it could be speculated that employment opportunities and higher salaries are particularly motivating to the college educated single older working women. Levels of education and occupational status are highly correlated (p <.01). Forty-six percent of the college educated have a professional or managerial job, whereas only 6 percent of those with just high school education have this type of work. In contrast, 72 percent of those with high school education have technical, sales, service, and clerical jobs compared to 51 percent of the college educated women in the same category. Operators and fabricators comprise 22 percent of the high school sample and 3 percent of the college educated.

Level of education has a strong positive association (p<.01) with earnings: more education means more earnings, which is not so highly correlated for men. Over one-quarter of those with only high school education earn less than $5,000 compared to 17 percent of the college educated. In the highest earnings categories, the high school educated comprise only 8 percent making more than $20,000 a year compared to 28 percent of the college educated.

Race

Eighty-six percent of the sample are White, 13 percent Black, and only 1 percent each are American Indian/Eskimo/Aleut or Asian/Pacific Islander. There are only 11 Hispanics in the sample. Because of small numbers, all minorities are combined into one "Non-White" category.

The White population working 18-34 hours is 5 percent more (91%) than the percent of Whites in the sample as a whole. On the other hand, in this same category of work hours non-Whites comprise 6 percent less (9%) than the total sample. There is no significance between work hours and race.

A more interesting finding is the percentage of non-Whites who work full time. Compared to 63 percent of Whites, 70 percent of non-Whites hold full-time jobs (Table 4.2). On the other hand, non-Whites work least (14%) in the 18-34 hour category, whereas Whites work least in the 1-17 hour subgroup.

Race is an important variable related to labor force participation patterns. However, because of small numbers of minorities in the sample, it is minimally considered in this research analysis.

Living Arrangements

Living arrangements refer to household composition, essentially living alone or living with others. As it relates to this research, the importance of this information is its relationship to the economic resources of single older working women. However, even though a relationship may or may not exist between living arrangements and economic wherewithal, women's decision to live alone or with others may be a life style choice based on a preference for companionship or for privacy more than on financial circumstances. The research data here only allows for an analysis of economic resources, not life style preferences.

The total percent of single working women living alone (57 percent) is higher than those living with others and remains so regardless of the number of hours worked (Table 4.1). In fact, according to the data, the likelihood of living alone increases as the number of working hours decreases—from 53 percent for full-time workers to 65 percent for less than half-time workers. For part timers, the percentage of difference between those living alone and those living with others is significant, with as much as a 30 percent gap between the two for those working less than half time. In contrast, full timers show a spread much less wide (only 6 percent) between the two categories of living arrangements: 53 percent living alone compared to 47 percent living with others. In describing the percentage distribution of hours worked by living arrangements (Table 4.2), the largest percent of those both living alone and living with others are full timers: 60 percent and 69 percent respectively.

Most single older working women, whether or not they are sharing resources, have limited earnings and total incomes. The salaries of those living alone are spread throughout the earnings categories, somewhat more weighted at the lower end with 45 percent making less than $7,560 a year and 61 percent making less than $12,000 a year (Table 4.4). The mid-range earnings category (with the least representation of those living alone) has the highest percentage of those living with others: 16 percent living alone compared to 28 percent living with others. As a result, contrary to what one might assume, single older women who live with others are significantly more likely (p<.05) to have higher earnings.

Table 4.4 Percent Distribution of Annual Earnings by Living Arrangements **

Sample Size: 395	(n=224)	(n=171)
	Living Alone	Living with Others
Annual Earnings		
≤ $ 3,600	22	19
$3,601 - $7,560	23	15
$7,561 - $12,000	16	28
$12,001 - $17,530	18	19
≥ $17,531	21	19

Source: Author's Tabulation of U.S. Bureau of the Census, Survey of Income and Program Participation (SIPP), Wave IV, 1984.
** p<.05

Non-earned income for both those living alone and those living with others (not in Table) is heavily weighted in the lowest non-earned income category of less than $665 per year, with the remainder in each group equally divided among the higher three non-earned income categories. When the total income is considered that includes both earnings and non-earnings (not in Table), there is a fairly even spread throughout the income categories for those both living alone and living with others, with approximately the same percentage having the least and having the most income. Unlike the relationship between living arrangements and earnings where there is a p<.05 level of significance, the relationship between living arrangements and both non-earned and total income is not significant. In other words, it makes no important real difference in single older working women's living arrangements if they have more or less non-earned or total income. Yet, contrary to what one might assume, if they live with someone else, their earnings are significantly higher (p<.05).

Another way to look at this data is that 47 percent living with others, yet working full time (Table 4.1), is relatively high and consistent with the reasons that older women work in the first place. One would expect that single older women have on average strong economic need and more reason to pool economic resources. Over three-fifths (62 percent) of the sample living with others make less than $12,000 a year.

Regions

Regions are grouped by states into four areas of the country based upon Bureau of the Census categories: Northeast, Midwest, South, and West. It is hypothesized that residential location may affect older women's job opportunities, including both hours of work and types of employment as well as earnings income.

As shown in Table 4.1, the South employs more single older women (33 percent) overall and in both the 1-17 hour (39 percent) and 35+ hour (33 percent) categories. The breakdown among all four regions is essentially the same overall and in the full-time category; the variation between the total sample and the full-time group for each region is no more than one percentage point. The largest range in working hours among regions exists in the 1-17 hour category, ranging from 15 percent in the West to 39 percent in the South.

Across categories of hours worked, the West employs the fewest single older women by far: 15 percent in the 1-17 hour category, 16 percent in the 35+ hour category, and 19 percent in the 18-34 hour group. In contrast, taking a look at the remaining three regions, the Northeast has the lowest percentages in the two part-time categories (23 percent at 1-17 hours and 25 percent at 18-34 hours), and the Midwest is lowest in the full-time category at 23 percent.

Interestingly, when analyzing hours worked in each region (Table 4.2), full-time workers are overrepresented in every region with a range of 60 to 68 percent of the total. On the other hand, in the less than half time category, each region is underrepresented with a range of 13 to 19 percent of the total. Within the 18-34 hour category there is a slightly higher percentage in each regional category except the South but only a seven point variation among regions, with the South having the least (17 percent) and the Midwest the most (24 percent).

Because of the unusually high level of consistency among regions in each category of hours worked compared to the distribution of the total sample, there is no statistical significance at all between regions and hours worked. Women in all regions seem to strongly favor full-time employment and to engage least often in less than half time work.

SUMMARY OF FINDINGS: DEMOGRAPHIC CHARACTERISTICS

The demographic variables with the strongest relationship to working hours are age and marital status. The "younger" a single woman's age among the older age categories, the more likely she is to work full time. The older her age, the more likely she is to work part time and to collect Social Security benefits.

Among different groups of single women, widows are by far the largest subgroup most represented in every category of working hours (i.e., 1-17 hours, 18-34 hours, and ≥35 hours). Yet, of their total number, they have the smallest percent working full time, which still amounts to over half (55 percent). In contrast, almost four-fifths (79 percent) of divorced older working women work full time.

Of the remaining demographic variables, there is no statistical significance between working hours and education, race, living arrangements, or regions. Because of a wide range of salaries and wages, earnings, unlike working hours, does demonstrate strong statistical significance with education: college education contributes to higher earnings. Also, like earnings, occupational status is highly correlated with education: almost one-half (46 percent) of the college educated have professional or managerial jobs. Because of the underrepresentation of minorities in the sample, specifically of Asians and Hispanics, race (a significant variable that influences secondary labor market participation) is only minimally considered in this analysis.

No statistical association between working hours and regional location may suggest a balance between supply and demand factors affecting both hours of work and the industrial mix in each region. Living arrangements also make no significant difference in working hours. It is curious that the largest percentage of those living alone are women working the least number of hours (1-17) with predominantly low earnings and limited total incomes.

EMPLOYMENT VARIABLES

There are certain employment factors that seem particularly related to hours of work. Among them, occupation is perhaps the most salient, since job type, one would speculate, is correlated with opportunities for part-time and full-time employment. It is also important to assess the degree to which this part-time work is voluntary, which this research data is able to determine. Also, because the availability of employee benefits, primarily health insurance and private pensions, are no longer "fringe," but rather are substantial inclusions in an employee's total earnings, employer (or union) provided health and pension plans may be particularly relevant to hours of work. Furthermore, whether a work setting is public or private (i.e., company type) may have bearing on the proportion of full-time versus part-time jobs. The last employment variable from the data set that may have a relationship to working hours is work site size, since the number of employees in one work location may have bearing upon the flexibility of working hours.

Occupation

Because of the large number of separate occupations among survey respondents, occupations are categorized into three primary groups that correspond to the U.S. Bureau of Labor Statistics headings: (1) professional and managerial; (2) technical, sales, service, (including private household), and clerical/administrative support; and (3) operators and fabricators. These three categories are often addressed as white collar, pink collar, and blue collar occupations.

There is high statistical significance between occupation and working hours (p<.01). As expected, the technical, sales, service, and administrative support category comprises more than half of the entire sample (67 percent), with the remaining sample fairly evenly split between professional and managerial (15 percent) and operators and fabricators (17 percent). Among the full-time category (Table 4.5), technical, sales, service, and administrative support represents a smaller percent (59 percent) than in the total sample (67 percent), yet three times more than either of the other two occupational groups. Both professionals/managers and operators/fabricators are more heavily represented in the full-time category than in the total sample: 19 percent and 22 percent respectively. In contrast, in both part-time categories, technical, sales, service, and administrative support represents an overwhelming majority: 81 percent for both 1 to 17 hours and 18 to 34 hours. The five occupational classifications with the highest concentrations in the sample all fall within this category: all sales (11 percent), secretary (10 percent), food preparation (9 percent), financial and material records (9 percent), and household worker (7 percent).

Interestingly, 79 percent of the small number of professional/managerial women work full time (Table 4.6), whereas only 56 percent of technical, sales, service, or administrative support women work full time. This finding is supported by other recent research that correlates full-time work with professional/managerial and least female-dominated jobs (Spalter-Roth and Hartmann, 1992). One might arrive at the conclusion that single older women with more "professional" jobs are more likely to work more hours except for the fact that operators and fabricators (blue collar workers) are also more likely to work full time (80 percent). Between the two part-time categories there is essentially no difference in the professional/managerial group (10 and 11 percent), relatively little difference in the technical, sales, service, and administrative support group (19 percent for 1 to 17 hours and 25 percent for 18 to 34 hours), with the same 6 percent variation in the operators/fabricators group (7 percent for 1 to 17 hours and 13 percent for 18 to 34 hours).

When occupations are analyzed according to age (not shown in Tables), clearly the youngest age range (55-61) has the largest percent of all three categories of workers: 59 percent of professionals/managers; 56 percent of technical, sales, service, and administrative support; and 71 percent of operators/fabricators. Interestingly, the percent of those in the technical, sales, service, and administrative support category drops drastically between ages 62 and 64 to 12 percent and then increases again to 18 percent at ages 65-69 and 14 percent after age 70. One could speculate from this finding that there is less incentive, whether it be financial gain or job satisfaction, that keeps this category of worker employed after age 62; availability of Social Security benefits may be more attractive for this lower paid worker who probably suffers less of a benefit penalty than a worker in the other two occupational categories, especially professionals and managers.

Table 4.5 Percent Distribution of Employment Characteristics by Hours Worked[a]

Sample Size: 395

	(n=63)	(n=79)	(n=253)	(n=395)
	Hours Worked			
	1-17	18-34	> 35	All
*Occupation***				
Professional/Managerial	11	7	19	15
Tech/Sales/Service/Adm Sup	81	81	59	67
Operators/Fabricators	8	11	22	17
*Employer/Union Pd Hlth Ins***				
NIU/None	77	68	19	38
All	16	21	43	34
Part	6	11	39	28
*Employer Pension Plan***				
No	90	77	46	59
Yes	10	23	54	41
*Company Type***				
Private	90	84	77	80
Public	10	16	23	20
*Work Site Size***				
< 25	77	58	31	44
25-99	13	19	25	22
100-499	10	23	43	34

Source: Author's Tabulation of U.S. Bureau of the Census, Survey of Income and Program Participation (SIPP), Wave IV, 1984.

[a]Percentages may not add up to 100 due to rounding.
***$p<.01$
** $p<.05$

Table 4.6 Percent Distribution of Hours Worked by Employment Characteristics[a]

Sample Size: 395

	Hours Worked			
	1-17	18-34	> 35	All (395)
*Occupation***				
Professional/Managerial	11	10	79	100 (61)
Tech/Sales/Service/Adm Sup	19	25	56	100 (264)
Operators/Fabricators	7	13	80	100 (70)
*Employer/Union Paid Health Insurance***				
NIU/None	32	37	31	100 (150)
All	7	13	80	100 (135)
Part	4	8	88	100 (110)
*Employer Pension Plan***				
No	24	26	50	100 (234)
Yes	4	12	84	100 (161)
*Company Type***				
Private	18	21	61	100 (317)
Public	8	17	76	100 (78)
*Work Site Size***				
< 25	28	27	45	100 (175)
25-99	9	17	73	100 (86)
100-499	4	14	81	100 (134)

Source: Author's Tabulation of U.S. Bureau of the Census, Survey of Income and Program Participation (SIPP), Wave IV, 1984.

[a]Percentages may not add up to 100 due to rounding.

***p<.01

** p<.05

Employer/Union Paid Health Insurance

This variable takes a look at the availability of health insurance by the respondent's employer or union. Of those who are offered health insurance, the question measures whether this insurance is paid for partially, fully, or not at all by the employer or union.

There is strong statistical significance (p<.01) between employer/union paid health insurance and working hours. Of the total sample, 62 percent have their employers or unions paying all or part of their health insurance. Of the full-time workers in Table 4.5, over four-fifths (82 percent) have their insurance totally (43 percent) or partially (39 percent) paid for by their employers or unions. In contrast, of the part-time workers, 32 percent of those working more than half time and 22 percent of those working less than half time, have employers or unions paying all or part of their health insurance. Access to and payment of health insurance may be a big incentive to working, especially full time. Or, it may simply be a reflection of working full time, since the coverage of full-time workers in this study is similar to the national average of 81 percent (EBRI Tabulations, Piacentini and Cerino, p. 173). However, this percentage is of all full-year, full-time workers, not just of women whose benefits are traditionally less than men's. According to a descriptive analysis of self-employed and part-time women workers that utilizes data from the 1986 and 1987 panels of the Survey of Income and Program Participation, women in full-time, full-year jobs are covered for fewer months than men in comparable jobs: 10.2 months for male workers, compared with 9.6 months for female workers (Spalter-Roth and Hartmann, 1992).

In describing the distribution of hours worked by availability and/or payment of health insurance by either the employer or the union (Table 4.6), it is noteworthy that 80 percent of those with full premium subsidies work full time and 88 percent with partial subsidies work full time. Also, almost three-quarters of those under age 65 have health insurance coverage at work, (not shown in Table). After age 65, when Medicare becomes available, only 31 percent of the sample receive employer paid health insurance.

Also, there is a high statistically significant relationship ($p < .01$) between health insurance and pensions provided by the employer, (not shown in Table). Forty-two percent of those with a retirement plan have partial payment of their health insurance and another 50 percent have their health insurance paid in full. Only 8 percent of those with retirement plans have no health insurance provided by their employer.

Employer Pension Plan

This variable looks at the availability of a pension plan provided by the employer. The survey asks if a plan is provided; responses are calculated based upon answers of either yes or no. While pension availability can be measured with this data set, there is no way of determining how many are actually eligible to receive a pension by having met vesting requirements, what type of pension plan is available, and how much the pension is worth.

Just over two-fifths of the sample and over half of the full-time workers have a retirement plan at work (Table 4.5). On the other hand, a large percent of the sample working part time in either category do not have an employer pension plan: 90 percent working 1-17 hours and 77 percent working 18-34 hours.

Eighty-four percent of those with a pension plan work full time, compared to 50 percent without a plan (Table 4.6). Access to a retirement plan certainly seems to strongly affect the level of labor force participation (p<.01), although the reverse (i.e., the relationship of working full time with the availability of a retirement plan) does not hold true to the same degree.

Of those who have a retirement plan at work, only 9 percent also collect Social Security benefits of no more than $5,000 annual, (not shown in Table). In relation to age, there is high statistical significance (p <.01) between the availability of employer provided pension plans and the age of the employee; as age increases, the percent of those with a pension plan decreases: 51 percent of 55-61 year olds, 43 percent of 62-64 year olds, 27 percent of 65-69 year olds, and 8 percent of those 70 years old and older (Table 4.7). This finding suggests that older single women who remain in the workforce do so because they cannot rely on any or much pension income and therefore have to work for financial reasons. Also, these results could signify different jobs in various age groups that have more or less access to employer pension plans.

Company Type

Company type refers to employment by either a private business or a public institution. Self employment is a third category of this variable that is deleted from the main content of this analysis because of missing information in this category. The skip pattern of the survey instrument contributed to the omission of certain information about the self-employed, primarily their occupations. In other words, if the respondents were self-employed, the interviewers skipped over questions related to occupation.

There is statistical significance (p<.05) between company type and working hours. Eighty percent of single older working women, regardless of working hours, work for private companies (Table 4.5).Twenty percent of the total sample work for the government, and a slightly larger percentage working full time are public employees. Of those working part time, an unusually high percentage work in private companies: 90 percent working 1-17 hours and 84 percent working 18-34 hours. In other words, the likelihood of working less than full time is much greater in the private than in the public sector.

Table 4.7 Percent Distribution of Employment Characteristics by Age[a]

Sample Size: 395	(n=234)	(n=51)	(n=59)	(n=51)
	Age			
	55-61	62-64	65-69	> 70
*Occupation*****				
Professional/Managerial	15	18	17	12
Tech/Sales/Service/Adm Sup	63	63	80	75
Operators/Fabricators	22	20	3	14
Employer/Union Pd Hlth Ins***				
NIU/None	25	31	61	78
All	43	27	19	20
Part	32	41	20	2
Employer Pension Plan***				
No	49	57	73	92
Yes	51	43	27	8
Company Type*				
Private	81	75	73	92
Public	19	25	27	8
Work Site Size***				
< 25	37	33	54	76
25-99	24	16	24	14
100-499	38	51	22	10

Source: Author's Tabulation of U.S. Bureau of the Census, Survey of Income and Program Participation (SIPP), Wave IV, 1984.

[a]Percentages may not add up to 100 due to rounding.
***p<.01
** p<.05
* p<.10

As expected, of the public employees in the sample (Table 4.6), over three-quarters work full time, compared to 61 percent of the private company subgroup. Of the private employees, a greater percent than in the public sector work varying amounts of part time: 39 percent as compared to 25 percent. These findings support the assumption that private companies are able to offer more flexibility in work hours.

Work Site Size

Work sites are specific facilities owned and operated by one company. The size of a work site may reflect the size of an entire company if it is the only company firm, or it may be one of several firms where more local business practices and policies are set and followed. There is a wide range in size among these sites: (1) less than 25, (2) between 25 and 99, and (3) between 100 and 499.

Over two-fifths of the total sample work in settings that employ fewer than 25 people. As illustrated in Table 4.5, in both part-time categories, but primarily in the 1 to 17 hours per week subgroup, the largest percentages are employed in work sites of less than 25: 77 percent working less than half time and 58 percent working more than half time. It is interesting to note, however, that the largest percentage of full-time workers (43 percent) are employed in sites of 100 to 499. There is a high level of significance ($p<.01$) between the size of the work site and the hours of work. As in the case of a private company, a firm with fewer than 25 employees has more flexibility to offer part time employment, especially the possibility of less than half time work.

Reasons for Part-Time Work

As mentioned previously, full-time employment is generally considered the standard (or default) for all workers, regardless of age or sex. The part-time workers represent altogether 36 percent of the working data set. An additional 4 percent (n=6) answer that they work full time, which probably means that they have two part-time jobs that amount to at least 35 hours of work per week.

When workers are not employed full time, according to this data set, there are reasons for working part time that are either voluntary or involuntary in nature. Voluntary part timers (70 percent of the part-time workforce) answer that they want part-time work or have normal working hours of less than 35 hours. Involuntary part timers (26 percent, with the remaining 4 percent responding "other") respond to the survey question in one of three ways: (1) they cannot find a full-time job; (2) there is slack work or material shortage; or (3) their health condition or disability prevents their working full time.

When looking at the relationship between voluntary/involuntary employment and age (Table 4.8), there is also high statistical significance (p <.01). Sixty-nine percent of the involuntary part-time workers are the "youngest" older workers between ages 55 and 61, who represent altogether only 38 percent of the part-time workforce. In contrast, most voluntary part timers are older than 65 (62 percent), which is 11 percent more than their overall percentages in the part-time labor force. It makes sense that part-time work would be voluntary if there are other sources of income, specifically Social Security benefits at age 65 and beyond; in fact, the hours would probably be kept low enough to remain within the income ceiling ($5,600 per individual in 1984) allowed by Social Security before the benefits are partially penalized. However, being forced into part-time work at a "younger" age (55-61) when there are no other financial resources can be an enormous economic hardship. At the p<.05 level of significance, marital status, education, company type (private or public), and work site size are associated with voluntary/involuntary employment. Widows, as the largest category of single women, comprise most of the voluntary and involuntary workforce, yet the percentage of voluntary (68 percent) is greater than the representation of all widows in the part-time labor force (61 percent). On the other hand, divorced and separated women are overrepresented in involuntary employment: 31 percent and 12 percent respectively compared to 18 percent and 5 percent of these single women in any kind of part-time work. Divorced and separated women, like the 55 to 61 year olds, are more likely than most widows to have no or few other financial resources other than their work; therefore, not being able to find full-time work contributes to their economic vulnerability.

In terms of education, the percentages of voluntary part-time workers closely correspond to the overall percentages of part-time workers. Among the involuntary workers, there is a slight overrepresentation of them among the less educated with high school education or less: 93 percent, compared to 84 percent in the overall part-time labor force. This finding is predictable, since level of education is related to the choice of working part-time: the more educated, the more voluntary and the less educated, the less voluntary.

As demonstrated in Table 4.9, while most part-time workers choose their hours of employment voluntarily, a sizable percent of part time workers, particularly those working 18-34 hours, would have preferred full- time jobs. Health problems account for only 1 percent of the part-time workforce and 4 percent of the involuntary workforce specifically.

As expected, there is high statistical significance (p <.01) between hours worked and voluntary/involuntary part-time employment. In other words, more labor force participation (i.e., more than half-time work) is associated positively with voluntary part-time employment. However, at the same time, there is much more likelihood of involuntary part-time employment among those working more than half time but less than full time: 43 percent compared to 26 percent working less than half time and 31 percent working full time as a result of combining part-time jobs. It appears that the more than half-time workers, who amount to just over half of the total part-time workforce, represent two dichotomous populations: those who like the hours they work and those who do not and prefer working full time.

There is also high statistical significance (p <.01) between voluntary/involuntary part-time work and occupation. As with the 18-34 hour-per-week workers, the largest percentages by far of both the voluntary and involuntary part-time workers fall within one subcategory; the technical/sales/service/administrative support area represents 83 percent voluntary and 64 percent involuntary, 6 percent more and 13 percent less respectively than the total percentage of this group of workers in the part-time labor force. Because the supply of service-related jobs often exceeds the demand, it is expected that service workers are more likely to be voluntary workers. And, it is also expected, yet for different reasons, that professionals and managers are more voluntary; with more education and skilled occupations that contribute to higher salaries, these workers have more choice of the hours that they work as well as less financial need to work full time. On the other hand, operators and fabricators are substantially overrepresented in the involuntary labor pool: 33 percent involuntary compared to 15 percent in the overall part-time workforce.

Table 4.8 Percent Distribution of Demographic Characteristics
by Voluntary and Involuntary Part-Time Work[a]

Sample Size: 153

	Part-Time Work		
	Voluntary (111)	Involunt-ary (42)	All (153)
Age***			
55-61	25	69	38
62-64	13	10	11
65-69	33	7	26
≥ 70	29	14	25
Marital Status**			
Widowed	68	45	61
Divorced	13	31	18
Separated	3	12	5
Never Married	17	12	16
Education**			
Some High School	41	48	42
High School Graduate	41	45	42
Some College	13	5	13
College Graduate	2		1
Post-College	4	2	3
Race			
White	91	77	86
Non-White	9	23	14
Living Arrangements			
Living Alone	65	55	62
Living with Others	35	45	38
Regions			
Northeast	25	24	25
Midwest	27	26	26
South	31	33	32
West	16	17	18

Source: Author's Tabulation of U.S. Bureau of the Census, Survey of Income and Program Participation (SIPP), Wave IV, 1984.

[a] Percentages may not add up to 100 due to rounding.
***p<.01
** p<.05

Although there is a high percentage of both voluntary and involuntary workers in private companies (given that most single older working women are employed in the private sector), the most striking finding is that among the involuntary part-time workers, 98 percent are employed in private companies. This almost universal amount represents 10 percentage points more than their total in the entire sample.

Like company type, work site size and voluntary/involuntary part-time work are significantly related (p<.05). Small work sites with fewer than 25 employees comprise more than half of both the voluntary and involuntary part-time workforce. While the smaller work sites are more likely to support voluntary part-time employment, the largest work sites of 100 to 499 employees have an overrepresentation of involuntary part timers: 26 percent compared to 21 percent of part-time workers overall in the total sample employed in the largest sites.

Voluntary/involuntary part-time work is associated, yet less strongly (p<.10), with employer provided pension plans and employer paid health insurance. It is interesting to note that of the total part-time labor force of single older women, there is an overrepresentation of voluntary workers who receive neither health insurance nor pension plans. The percentage of involuntary part timers—with or without pension plans—is approximately equal in number to the total part-time sample (30 percent with pension plans and involuntary and 70 percent with no pension plan and voluntary). Yet, these same involuntary part-time workers with health insurance coverage are overrepresented by 13 percentage points in the total sample. Even with access to health insurance, there are still many more part-time workers who prefer working full time. And, those without health insurance are almost three-quarters voluntary part-time workers (73 percent). From these findings, one might assume that health insurance is only one reason that single older women work full time. It appears as if they work more hours primarily for the money.

Table 4.9 Percent Distribution of Employment
Characteristics by
Voluntary and Involuntary Part-Time Work[a]

Sample Size: 153

	Part-Time Work		
	Volunt- ary (111)	Invol- untary (42)	All
Hours Worked***			
1-17	45	26	39
18-34	55	43	51
≥ 35		31	10
Occupation***			
Professional/Managerial	10	2	8
Tech/Sales/Service/Adm Sup	83	64	77
Operators/Fabricators	7	33	15
Employer/Union Pd Hlth Ins*			
NIU/None	73	52	66
All	17	33	23
Part	10	14	11
Employer Pension Plan*			
No	83	71	70
Yes	17	29	30
Company Type**			
Private	84	98	88
Public	16	2	12
Work Site Size**			
< 25	67	57	63
25-99	17	17	16
100-499	16	26	21

Source: Author's Tabulation of U.S. Bureau of the Census, Survey of Income and
Program Participation (SIPP), Wave IV, 1984.

[a]Percentages may not add up to 100 due to rounding.
***p<.01
** p<.05
*   p<.10

SUMMARY OF FINDINGS: EMPLOYMENT CHARACTERISTICS

Working hours are strongly associated with all of the employment variables chosen for this study (p<.01 except for company type at p<.05). Two-thirds of the sample work in technical, sales, service, and administrative support jobs, and four-fifths of those working both less and more than half time are in those jobs. Although the remaining sample are almost equally divided between professionals/managers and operators/fabricators, four-fifths of each of these subgroups work full time.

And, 80 to 88 percent of full-time workers have their health insurance completely or partially paid by their employer or union; this represents 18 to 26 percentage points more than their overall percentage in the total sample. In contrast, of the part-time workers, only 36 percent of the sample, only between 12 and 20 percent have employer health insurance partially or totally subsidized. More single older women have paid health insurance than retirement plans from their jobs. Only 54 percent of full-time workers have private pension plans from work, yet of the total sample covered by these plans over four-fifths are full-time workers. It is interesting to note that as the working hours of these women increase, the percentage of those with retirement plans decreases. This finding further supports the economic rationale for continued labor force participation among those with little or no non-earned income.

Full-time employment is much more likely (p<.01) in larger (100-499 employees) than smaller sites. The smallest sites of 25 or less, representing less than half of the total sample, have many more single older women working part time, especially less than half time.

Because of the growing number of contingent, involuntary part-time workers, it is important to determine the factors that determine working part time among single older women. As expected, the "youngest" single older women have the largest percentage (69) of involuntary part timers. Widows, with the largest number of part timers in the sample, also have the largest percentage of voluntary workers. Divorce, although less than one-fifth of the part-time sample, represents almost one-third of involuntary workers. The more educated the women (i.e., with at least some college), the more voluntary are the part-time workers. Almost all of the part-time professionals and managers are voluntary. Part-time technical/sales/service/administrative support workers are more voluntary than involuntary, and part-time operators/fabricators are mostly involuntary.

To a lesser degree (p<.05), work site size is associated with voluntary/involuntary part-time work. Whereas small sites (less than 25 employees) include a large proportion (over half) of both voluntary and involuntary single older women workers, the largest sites of 100+ employees (with only one-fifth of the part-time sample) have an overrepresentation of involuntary part timers.

Employer paid health insurance and employer provided pension plans are significantly related (p<.10) to voluntary/involuntary part-time work. Almost three-quarters of voluntary part timers receive no employer paid health insurance, and almost one half of the involuntary part timers do receive insurance. Part timers without pension plans, like those without health insurance, are overrepresented in the voluntary part-time labor force.

Descriptive statistics clearly indicate that there are more employment than demographic characteristics closely associated with working hours. In addition to age and marital status, determinants of working hours are primarily occupation, employer or union paid health insurance, employer pension plans, work site size, reason for part-time work (voluntary or involuntary), and company type (public or private).

For most demographic and employment variables, working part time rather than full time is more relevant than the number of part-time hours—i.e., less than versus more than half time. The profiles of less than half-time workers tend to be more single women 70 years of age and older, mostly white, widowed, with less than a high school diploma, living alone, predominantly in the South. They primarily work in pink collar jobs without health insurance or pension plans from work and in private companies with less than 25 employees.

On the other hand, more than half-time workers are in the youngest age category of 55 to 61 years of age, with a smaller percentage of widows living alone than the less-than-half timers, yet with a larger percentage of whites who are high school graduates living in the Midwest. These more than half-time workers are very similar occupationally to less than half-time workers, yet they have a larger proportion with paid health insurance and pension plans from work who are employed somewhat less often in private companies and in the smallest work sites. The voluntary/involuntary status of their part-time work is especially relevant: Those working 18-34 hours represent more of both the voluntary and involuntary part-time workforces as well as the involuntary full-time workforce. These findings imply, perhaps, that less than half-time workers, although they may have more flexibility of working fewer hours, especially in small work sites in private companies, represent more of the marginal workers in the secondary labor market, who are older, less educated, unskilled, and unprotected by employee benefits. The relationship between hours of work and income variables, discussed in Chapter 5, provides additional data about the economic status of part-time workers and the economic differences between those working 1-17 hours versus those working 18-34 hours as they compare to full-time workers.

ANALYSIS OF VARIANCE

As described in Chapter 3, analysis of variance (ANOVA) serves the purpose of determining the relative significance of the explanatory variables on the dependent variable, hours of work. This statistical method offers three research opportunities: (1) it disaggregates the portion of variation in mean hours worked that is related to one of the interval variables, specifically working hours or income factors, (2) it provides the statistical difference in mean hours worked between important categorical explanatory variables, such as some of the demographic and employment variables described earlier in this chapter, and (3) it automatically looks for any interactions between these categories along with main effects. In three additional ANOVAs, analyzed in Chapter 5, hours of work is considered as one of several *independent* variables that have an effect on three income aggregates: mean total annual earnings, non-earnings, and overall income. The ANOVA of mean hours worked (Table 4.10) suggests that women are much more likely to work full time at younger ages (55-61) where there is access to employer paid health insurance. Occupation and work site size are also associated with hours of work (p<.05); service-related jobs in small work sites offer the widest range of working hours—that is, the most opportunity to work part time.

Mean Hours Worked

There is high overall statistical significance (p<.01) of the average hours worked when controlling for the sources of variation considered most relevant in this research study: marital status, age, education, occupation, health insurance, employer pensions, work site size, hourly wage, and household wealth (Table 4.10). Average hours worked differ at the p<.01 level by age and employer provided health insurance, at the p<.05 level by occupation, and at the p<.10 level by work site size. The other categorical independent variables have no statistical significance on mean hours worked.

It is no surprise that age is strongly associated with the number of hours worked: the younger the age of single older women, the more likely these women are to work more hours. This association is probably related to several factors: better health, higher energy, more job opportunities, negligible access to public or private pensions before ages 62 or 65, and more interest in work over leisure. Also, it is no surprise that occupation is associated with hours worked, even though the association is not so strong as with age. Service occupations offer most flexibility of hours, with the largest percentages by far working in this area regardless of working hours. Another way of describing this association is that full-time workers represent the largest percentage in all three occupation categories.

Work site size, though less significant (p<.10), has bearing upon working hours: the larger the work site, the more likelihood of working full time. The greatest range of hours seems to occur in the smallest work sites of fewer than 25 employees, where there is an almost even split between those working full time and those working less than half time. One can reasonably conclude that the increasing possibility of working less than half time in small work sites indicates greater flexibility than larger employers in some cases, and suggests poorer job opportunities in other cases.

Table 4.10 ANOVA of Mean Hours Worked: Working Women

Source of Variation[b]	F-Statistic	Significance
Marital Status	.727	.536
Age	10.693	.000***
Education	.853	.492
Occupation	3.926	.021**
Employer/Union Pd Hlth Ins	8.644	.000***
Work Site Size	2.339	.098*
Employer Pension Plan	.665	.415
Hourly Wage	.396	.812
Household Wealth	.169	.954
Total Explained Variation	*6.881*	*.000***

Source: Author's Tabulation of U.S. Bureau of the Census, Survey of Income and Program Participation (SIPP), Wave IV, 1984.

[b]Except for education, only the explanatory variables that demonstrate statistic significance in chi squares are included in the ANOVA.

***p<.01   ** p<.05   * p<.10

Work site size, though less significant (p<.10), has bearing upon working hours: the larger the work site, the more likelihood of working full time. The greatest range of hours seems to occur in the smallest work sites of fewer than 25 employees, where there is an almost even split between those working full time and those working less than half time. One can reasonably conclude that the increasing possibility of working less than half time in small work sites indicates greater flexibility than larger employers in some cases, and suggests poorer job opportunities in other cases.

An interesting finding is the positive association between hours worked and health insurance. Health insurance on the job is highly related to hours of work. Single women, particularly as they get older, have difficulty obtaining or choosing full-time work, and, therefore, the availability of health insurance is greatly reduced. This phenomenon speaks to the urgent need of protecting these women with health insurance at ages that precede Medicare eligibility. Without this protection, many of these older women may be forced to work full time beyond what they would otherwise choose to do. Health care reform, as designed by United States President Clinton, may provide just that protection, so that working—if and how much—becomes more of a choice.

COMPARISON GROUP

There is a notable contrast between the working single older women and the comparison group of non-working single older women. Compared to working women, the non-working women from this data set are generally much older, much more likely to be widowed, have significantly less education, and are somewhat more likely to live alone. Yet, the regional and racial composition of both groups are very similar. According to economic criteria, described in Chapter 5, the non-working sample has much in common with the working women. Both groups can be quite poor or rich; what insulates the working women from poverty are their earnings.

Demographic Comparison: Non-Working versus Working Women

Table 4.11 compares overall percentages of working and non-working women related to age, marital status, education, race, living arrangements, and regions. The non-working sample of older women is comprised of 2,166 as compared to 395 who are working—that is, almost 5 1/2 times more women.

The data demonstrates that marital status, education, and living arrangements are strongly associated with working or not working. Widows represent over three-quarters of the sample of non-working women. This statistic is expected since widows tend to be older and, therefore, less likely to work. It is less expected, however, that widowed single older women also represent the largest percentage of the working sample (50 percent). The other surprising finding is that divorced women are almost twice as likely as never married women to work, whereas women from those two marital status categories among the non-working are almost equal numbers.

Education more than race reflects the dual labor market theory. There is a much higher percentage of older non-working women with less than a high school education: 58 percent compared to 34 percent working. The largest percentage of working women are those who have completed high school (42 percent). An even larger percentage of the non-working are least educated. Whereas the less educated are more likely to not work, the more educated—with at least some college—are more likely to work. More education may allow for more job opportunities and more job satisfaction.

There are significant differences (p<.01) in the patterns of living arrangements between single older women who are working and not working. Although both working and non-working single older women are much more likely to live alone, there is even more likelihood of living alone among the non-working women. Given that living alone is more costly, these findings do not suggest relative financial comfort among the non-working (with 10 percent less total wealth). Hence, is this finding more indicative of life style preferences (with widows, as the highest percentage of non-working, preferring to live alone after their spouses die)? In reviewing the income variables, Chapter 5 may provide a partial answer to these questions.

Table 4.11 Percent Distribution of Demographic
Characteristics
by Working and Non-Working Women[a]

Sample Sizes	(n=395)	(n=2,166)
	Working	Non-Working
Age		
55-61	59	10
62-64	13	8
65-69	15	18
≥ 70	12	65
Marital Status***		
Widowed	50	77
Divorced	29	9
Separated	6	3
Never Married	15	11
Education***		
Some High School	34	58
High School Graduate	42	25
Some College	14	10
College Graduate	5	4
Post-College	5	4
Race		
White	86	87
Non-White	15	14
Living Arrangements***		
Living Alone	57	65
Living with Others	43	35
Regions		
Northeast	27	25
Midwest	24	22
South	33	37
West	16	16

Source: Author's Tabulation of U.S. Bureau of the Census, Survey of Income and
Program Participation (SIPP), Wave IV, 1984.
[a]Percentages may not add up to 100 due to rounding.
***p<.01

Age, primarily a proxy for the degree of labor force participation, is not significantly related to working or not. The youngest single older women work, and the oldest do not, with the smallest percentage of both working and not working between ages 62 and 64. It is interesting to note that in the 62 to 69 year old age ranges, when early or regular Social Security retirement apply as well as reduced retirement benefits between ages 62 and 65 and an income ceiling through age 69, an almost equal percentage of women continue working as do not work. This finding suggests that at the time of this data collection in 1984, the incentives to work (e.g., financial need or penalties for retiring early) are offset by the disincentives to work (e.g., Social Security benefits reduced by half related to exceeding the low earnings income ceiling or meager financial credits from working between ages 65 and 69).

Although age has no overall significance with working or not working, the percent of the total sample who work over age 70 is relatively and unexpectedly high. It is, therefore, useful to look at in more detail the demographic characteristics of these women by age as they compare with non-working women of the same age (Table 4.12). For both the working and non-working women, there is a strong association (p<.01) between age and marital status. The oldest single working women are almost three-quarters widows (73 percent). Widowed women represent an even higher percentage of the non-working women: over four-fifths (83 percent). Divorced women are much more representative of the working sample in the younger subgroups, particularly among 55-61 year olds. Never married women, on the other hand, although smaller in numbers, are more than double the size of divorcees working at age 70 or older.

Related to age, the other significant demographic variable for both the working and non-working samples, is living arrangements. Compared with working women, non-working women are more likely to live with others in the youngest age category and to live alone in the oldest age category. The relationship between age and living arrangements is stronger for non-working women (p<.01) than for working women (p<.10).

Table 4.12 Percent Distribution of Select Demographic Characteristics by Age: Working and Non-Working Women[a]

	Age			
	55-61	62-64	65-69	> 70
WORKING (n=395)	(234)	(51)	(59)	(51)
Marital Status***				
Widowed	40	51	71	73
Divorced	38	25	15	8
Separated	7	6	2	2
Never Married	15	18	12	18
Education				
Some High School	31	41	36	43
High School Graduate	45	37	37	33
Some College	12	10	20	16
College Graduate	6	4	3	2
Post-College	5	8	3	6
Living Arrangements*				
Living Alone	51	61	68	65
Living with Others	49	39	32	35
NON-WORKING (n=2,166)	(216)	(164)	(380)	(1406)
Marital Status***				
Widowed	56	67	72	83
Divorced	21	16	12	6
Separated	11	4	4	1
Never Married	12	13	12	11
Education***				
Some High School	56	51	48	61
High School Graduate	28	30	32	22
Some College	10	10	13	9
College Graduate	3	5	3	4
Post-College	3	4	4	4
Living Arrangements***				
Living Alone	48	63	67	67
Living with Others	52	37	33	33

Source: Author's Tabulation of U.S. Bureau of the Census, Survey of Income and Program Participation (SIPP), Wave IV, 1984.   ***p<.01
[a]Percentages may not add up to 100 due to rounding.   * p<.10

Education, on the other hand, is strongly associated with age (p<.01) for non-working women, yet not at all for working women. Clearly, the non-working women of all ages tend to be least educated, representing over three-fifths of the oldest non-working age category and only two-fifths of the oldest working sample. Among the working sample, the oldest are most
likely to have the least education, yet they represent a much smaller proportion of the whole than the least educated non-workers. The least educated women are by far most represented at every age level among the non-working women, in contrast to the high school graduates having more presence, particularly in the youngest age category, among working women.

There are no regional differences between those who do not work and those who do. With the race variable, the percentage of those working and not working are almost identical. In other words, race by itself is not related to working or not. This finding of no difference is somewhat surprising, since labor force discrimination against minorities results in sparse job opportunities, on the one hand, or increased financial need due to lower paying jobs, on the other. Perhaps, both factors that would contribute to more or less labor force participation cancel each other out.

SUMMARY OF FINDINGS: ANOVA OF MEAN HOURS WORKED AND DEMOGRAPHIC COMPARISON WORKING AND NON-WORKING WOMEN

Both the ANOVA of mean hours worked and the comparison between working and non-working single older women offer more refined, sophisticated analyses of single older working women. The ANOVA of mean hours worked indicates, while controlling for important independent variables, the strong association between working hours and age as well as access to paid employer/union health insurance. The younger the single older working woman (i.e., between ages 55 and 61), the more she is to work full time and receive employer/union paid health insurance. Age in many ways is a proxy for the extent of labor force participation, so that the correlation between working hours and age is not surprising. However, is employer/union paid health insurance also a proxy for working hours? Certainly, those who work more hours are more likely to receive health insurance on the job. What is hard to determine is the degree to which access to this health insurance serves as a strong motivator to work full time, even when one is older and, perhaps, less inclined to work full time for a variety of reasons.

Working hours, on the one hand, may be a measure of job flexibility, demonstrating the degree to which jobs are responsive to workers' needs. On the other hand, working hours may be more a measure of employers' needs that have contributed to a dual labor market and to a contingent, involuntary part-time workforce. Thus, in the ANOVA of mean hours worked, as one analyzes the significant association between working hours and both occupation and work site size, it is unclear what underlies the increasing amount of part-time work among single older women in service occupations and in small work sites. Are single older women in these jobs by choice, or are these jobs the only work that is available to them?

By comparing single older working women to their non-working counterparts, there is an additional barometer for highlighting what is special and different about single older working women. Widows represent one half of the working sample and over three-fourths of the non-working sample, probably because of increasing age among the non-workers. In contrast, probably related to younger ages, divorced single older women are more than three times more frequently represented in the working than the non-working sample. Concerning education, the single older women most likely not to work have only some high school education, and those most likely to work have a high school diploma. And, most surprising, single older women who do not work are more likely to live alone than those who do work: 65 percent compared to 57 percent. Because age is strongly associated with living arrangements and living alone is strongly associated with not working, it would follow that increasing age is associated with more likelihood of not working.

Demographic and employment variables offer only limited understanding of single older women and their labor force patterns. Because the labor force participation of single older women is heavily influenced by their economic needs, Chapter 5 will analyze the income factors that contribute to their working.

Chapter V

Income Findings

INCOME VARIABLES

The SIPP data set is rich with information about individual and household economic resources. In order to determine more fully the economic vulnerability of older single women in the workforce, the variables that seem most relevant to this analysis are: annual earnings income, hourly wage, annual non-earned income (i.e., income from assets, private pensions and Social Security benefits), total annual income, and total household wealth (primarily home equity).

Annual Earnings Income

As would be expected, single older women working full time, who are 64 percent of the total working sample, earn substantially more than those working part time: five times more than those working 1 to 17 hours weekly and almost three times more than those working 18 to 34 hours (Table 5.1). Earnings income represents 84 percent of the total income of full-time workers (Table 5.2). That proportion is 53 percent for women who work more than half time and 33 percent for those who work less than half time.

Table 5.1 Average Annual Income by Sources and Hours Worked[c]

Sample Size: 395

Source	1-17 Hours	18-34 Hours	> 35 Hours
Total Income	$9,584	$10,536	$18,356
Total Earnings	3,145	5,544	15,400
Total Non-Earned Inc	6,440	4,992	2,956

Source: Author's Tabulation of U.S. Bureau of the Census, Survey of Income and Program Participation (SIPP), Wave IV, 1984.
[c]Rounded to nearest dollar.

Table 5.2 Percent of Total Annual Income by Source and Hours Worked

Sample Size: 395   (n=62)   (n=81)   (n=252)

	Hours Worked		
Source	1-17 Hours	18-34 Hours	>35 Hours
Total Earnings	33	53	84
Total Non-Earned Inc	67	47	16

Source: Author's Tabulation of U.S. Bureau of the Census, Survey of Income and Program Participation (SIPP), Wave IV, 1984.

In order to divide the sample into essentially five equal subgroups, annual earnings range from less than or equal to $3,600 on the low end to a high of more than or equal to $17,531. Several of the independent variables in this research study have high statistical significance ($p < .01$) with annual earnings: age, education (Table 5.3), work hours, occupation, employer paid health insurance, company type, and work site size (Table 5.4). In other words, there is a strong relationship between a single employed older woman's total salary or pay and each of the above variables. What this means is that a "younger" older women (55-61 years of age), with at least a high school education, working full time, in white or pink collar jobs (professional/manager or technical/sales/service or administrative support), in large work sites (100-499 employees), in private companies, or where health insurance is partially or totally paid for and a pension plan is covered are most likely to show higher earnings (more than $12,000).

Single older working women in the youngest age group (55-61) are most represented in the $12,001-$17,530 range, not the highest earnings category. In the lowest two earnings categories, there is more of a spread in ages than in the upper three. In fact, single women making $3,601-$7,560 annually are almost as likely to be 55 to 61 years of age or 62 and older; this is clearly not the case in the three highest earnings categories where the 55 to 61 year olds represent approximately three-quarters of each earnings category. There is a larger representation of low earners between 65 and 69 years of age, whereas the earnings level of 62 to 64 year olds is more variable with a much less clear pattern across earnings categories. The oldest workers have the highest proportionate representation among the lowest earners, which, as discussed earlier, is partly related to reduced hours of work. In addition to fewer work hours, the oldest single working women are most likely to be employed in pink collar jobs where they primarily demonstrate least skills (Table 4.7).

As expected, sample women with less than a high school diploma represent the highest percent in the lowest earnings category. In the other four earnings categories, high school graduates are the largest subgroup. The percent significantly drops as earnings increase in the highest two earnings categories. Single women with at least a college degree represent 29 percent of the highest earnings category, with an additional 18 percent in this highest earnings bracket having some college education. In contrast, in the second highest earnings category, there are only 10 percent who have a college degree. Even in this cohort, where job opportunities have been limited, clearly college educated women have had a distinct advantage in their earnings power and their incentive to work.

Technical, sales, service, and administrative support workers are the most important group in every earnings category. Four-fifths of each of the two lowest earnings categories are in this occupational group, as compared to a progressive decline (69 percent, 53 percent, and 49 percent) in the remaining upper earnings categories. Although the largest percentage (34 percent) of professionals/managers are represented in the highest earnings category, the largest percentage in the highest earnings category represent the technical/sales/service/administrative support group.

Table 5.3 Percent Distribution of Demographic Characteristics by Annual Earnings[a]

Sample Size: 395

	Annual Earnings[d]				
	< $3,600	$3,601-$7,560	$7,561-$12,000	$12,001-$17,530	> $17,531
Age*					
55-61	22	53	73	78	72
62-64	12	9	15	12	15
65-69	25	28	6	5	10
≥70	41	10	6	4	3
Marital Status*					
Widowed	59	58	50	37	47
Divorced	16	22	35	36	37
Separated	5	8	6	7	3
Never Married	20	13	10	21	14
Education*					
Some High School	56	35	35	27	19
High School Graduate	27	51	51	44	34
Some College	9	10	14	18	18
College Graduate	4	1	0	5	15
Post-College	5	3	0	5	14
Race					
White	80	87	83	88	91
Non-White	19	13	16	12	9
Living Arrangements*					
Living Alone	60	67	43	55	59
Living with Others	40	33	57	45	41
Regions					
Northeast	21	23	25	33	32
Midwest	30	23	21	24	23
South	38	32	38	26	28
West	11	21	15	17	18

Source: Author's Tabulation of U.S. Bureau of the Census, Survey of Income and Program Participation (SIPP), Wave IV, 1984.

[a]Percentages may not add up to 100 due to rounding. ***p<.01
[d]Earnings divided into five equal quintiles. ** p<.05

Table 5.4 Percent Distribution of Employment
Characteristics by Annual Earnings[a]

Sample Size: 395

	Annual Earnings[d]				
	< $3,600	$3,601-$7,560	$7,561-$12,000	$12,00-$17,530	>$17,531
*Hours of Work****					
1-17	58	12	6	1	0
18-34	26	59	12	5	0
≥35	16	29	82	93	100
*Occupation****					
Professional/Managerial	11	4	7	22	34
Tech/Sales/Service/Adm Sup	80	81	69	53	49
Operators/Fabricators	9	15	24	25	16
*Health Insurance****					
NIU/None	79	62	35	8	4
All	16	18	36	42	59
Part	5	21	30	49	37
*Employer Pension Plan****					
No	91	76	67	41	19
Yes	9	24	33	59	81
*Company Type****					
Private	85	87	89	82	57
Public	15	13	11	18	43
*Work Site Size****					
<25	77	53	44	26	19
25-99	14	19	14	40	24
100-499	10	28	42	34	56

Source: Author's Tabulation of U.S. Bureau of the Census, Survey of Income and
Program Participation (SIPP), Wave IV, 1984.
[a]Percentages may not add up to 100 due to rounding.
[d]Earnings divided into five equal quintiles.
***p<.01

Professionals/managers comprise very small percentages in the lowest three earnings categories and only 22 percent in the second highest earnings category. Operators and fabricators are most represented at one-quarter in the third and fourth earnings categories, making between $7,561 and $17,530. There is an approximately equal percentage from this occupational group in the highest earnings category and in the second lowest. In other words, it appears as if blue collar single older women workers can be either low-level or high-level earners and probably represent a wide range of skilled and unskilled laborers.

It is noteworthy that in the highest two categories of earnings ($12,000+), 100 percent of the sample work full time and that in the next two lower categories ($7,561-$17,530), 93 percent and 82 percent respectively work full time. This reflects two different effects: hours worked and wage rates, (discussion to follow). The smallest percentage (16 percent) of full-time workers are in the lowest earnings category. Fifty-nine percent of those working 18-34 hours are at the lower end of the earnings scale, making $3,601-$7,560. The highest percentage (58 percent) of those working less than half time are in the lowest earnings category. There is no representation of those working less than or more than half time in the highest earnings category. Full-time workers, while skewed in the direction of higher earnings, are represented in all earnings categories with the smallest percentage (16 percent) in the lowest earnings category.

Employee benefits, primarily payment of health insurance and pension coverage, are significantly related to annual pay (p <.01). The higher the earnings, the more likely there is to be health insurance supplied by employers or unions and employer pension benefits. Ninety-six percent of the highest paid have health insurance, subsidized totally or partially by work. Insurance payments progressively decline as earnings decline. Yet, even in the lowest earnings category 21 percent of workers have paid health insurance from their employer. In each earnings category, however, pension plans do not reflect as high a percentage of coverage as paid health insurance: from a low of 9 percent earning the least to a high of 81 percent earning the most.

Private companies, that employ most single older women, offer both the least and the most annual earnings. However, the percentage differential in earnings between private and government jobs is by far the least at the highest level (≥$17,531). Private companies include over four-fifths of the sample in all but the highest earnings category; there is a 25 percentage point drop in private company representation between the second highest and the highest earnings categories.

Like private companies, the smallest work sites (of less than 25 employees) have the highest percentage of the lowest earners, and the largest work sites (of 100-499 employees) have the highest percentage of highest earners. It would follow, then, that single older women are most at risk economically if they work in very small private companies, (which, as demonstrated earlier, is a reflection of the proportion of part-time jobs).

Marital status and living arrangements are also associated with annual pay (p<.05). Widows are more represented in every earnings category, partly because widows are the largest group of single older working women. However, their percentage increases to over half in the two lowest earnings categories. And, they are least represented in the second highest earnings category, yet even here they have a 1 percent advantage over the next most represented marital group at this earnings level, divorced women. Among the divorcees, a larger proportion are represented in the three highest earnings categories. Never married women are spread throughout the earnings groups, contrary to the assumption that these women (compared to other single women) might have the strongest work histories—without time out of the labor force to raise children—and resulting highest earnings. Separated women also show a range of earnings, with the least making the most.

Although 57 percent of the total sample of single older working women live alone, it is interesting to note that they are more likely to live with others only in the middle earnings category and are most likely to live alone in the second lowest earnings category. These findings contradict common sense that single women with less earnings (and less total income) need to share expenses with "roommates."

Only race and regions show no significance with pay. Perhaps, the influence of race is subsumed under the variables of education and occupation, both of which are highly significant with annual pay.

Hourly Wage

Hourly wage offers a different measure of the "economic returns to working" than earnings and, as such, may be associated differently with working hours. As mentioned in Chapter 3, earnings, on the one hand, have an accounting relationship with hours and wages. That is, earnings=hours x wages. Wages, on the other hand, do not suffer from a tautological relationship with hours as earnings do. Unlike earnings, wages do not necessarily differ by the number of hours someone works; they differ for theoretical and behavioral reasons, not accounting ones.

Intuitively, one might assume that earnings and hourly pay have the same effect on working hours and that low (or high) earnings reflect low (or high) wages; in other words, wages increase progressively as hours increase. The research findings indicate that this is not the case.

The average hourly wage differs according to the category of hours worked. Among part-time workers, the larger mean hourly wage of $5.26 is for the lesser number of working hours (1-17). The lower mean hourly wage is $4.55 for sample women working more than half time, which is $.71 (or 13 percent) less than the women working the least number of hours. Full-time workers make $7.66 on average: $3.11 and $2.40 more per hour than those working less than and more than half time respectively. This difference in wages is significant; a variation of $3.11 between the highest and lowest average wage represents 41 percent.

On the one hand, one might expect a higher hourly wage for increased labor force participation, taking into consideration some lowered adjustment if employee benefits are included in the salary level. On the other hand, a higher hourly wage might be necessary to stimulate added demand for those working the least number of hours. Also, firms pay wages for different types of workers, differentiated by occupation, education, and experience; wages may vary based more on these demographic and employment characteristics than on hours of work.

What is most curious in the research findings is the significant drop in hourly wage of $.71 in the 18-34 hours of work category. This drop suggests more than an adjustment for the possible inclusion of benefits in the salary level, since full-time workers, with more likelihood of benefits, show a substantial increase in average hourly wage. Perhaps, there is a shift in the balance of supply and demand that indicates more supply and less demand of jobs with 18-34 hours as compared to 1-17 hours; this phenomenon may be particularly true for those women collecting Social Security benefits who want to stay within the income ceiling and thereby work fewer hours. Or, it may be that older single women who work more part-time hours have a different motivation to work other than making money (access to health and/or pension benefits, job satisfaction, or social contacts).

The data indicates, however, that when the sample is divided into five equal segments (<$3.69, $3.70-$5.03, $5.04-$6.62, $6.63-$9.17, >$9.18), 35 percent of those working less than half time and another 36 percent of those working more than half time earn the lowest amount of hourly wage (Table 5.5). And, except for the middle wage category, the 18-34 working hours subgroup represents the largest percentage making the least (<$3.69) or the smallest percentage making the most (>$6.63). Of those making the highest wage, 27 percent work full time. Only 11 percent of full-time workers are in the lowest wage category. In contrast, only 4 percent of those working more than half time and 11 percent of women working less than half time are included in the highest wage group. In other words, not only is the average hourly wage much higher for full-time workers but also the percentage of those making higher wages, especially the highest two wage categories, is much greater. The findings clearly demonstrate a very high level of significance at <.01 with the association between wage and working hours.

Table 5.5 Percent Distribution[a] of Hourly Wage by Hours Worked[e]

Sample Size: 389	(n=62)	(n=78)	(n=249)
	Hours Worked		
	1-17	18-34	>35
Hourly Wage[d]			
≤$3.69	35	36	11
$3.70-$5.03	24	31	15
$5.04-$6.62	15	19	22
$6.63-$9.17	15	10	24
≥$9.18	11	4	27

Source: Author's Tabulation of U.S. Bureau of the Census, Survey of Income and Program Participation (SIPP), Wave IV, 1984.

[a]Percentages may not add up to 100 due to rounding.
[d]Wages divided into five equal quintiles.
[e]Missing observations = 1.5%.

There is also a strong statistical relationship (p <.01) between wage level and age, education, occupation, and receipt of both health insurance and pensions from work (Table 5.6). Single women making higher wages tend to be in the youngest age category. The youngest older women are most represented in the second highest wage category (at 74 percent) and least represented in the lowest wage category (at 38 percent). On the other hand, the oldest single women (≥ 70 years old) are most represented in reverse: the most in the lowest wage category (32 percent) and the least in the second highest wage category (1 percent). In the 62-64 and 65-69 age groups, there is a more even spread throughout the wage categories, with the 62-64 year old women more likely to make higher wages and the 65-69 year olds more likely to make lower wages.

There is a strong positive association between education and wages. Women earning the lowest wage are most likely to have the least education; 60 percent of those with less than a high school degree earn ≤$3.69. High school graduates, representing the largest education subgroup in the sample (42 percent), are less than half as likely as those without a high school degree to earn the lowest wage. Most high school graduates earn wages in the middle three wage categories. Although single women with at least some college education represent only approximately one-quarter of the total sample, they are much more likely to earn higher wages, with 46 percent combined in the highest wage group.

The largest percentage of white collar workers make the highest wage (40 percent of the total sample, which amounts to 51 percent of professionals and managers). The largest percentage of pink collar workers are in the two lowest wage categories, representing at least three-quarters of the total sample, altogether equaling 47 percent of their entire number in the sample. Blue collar workers are most represented in the middle wage category at 28 percent, which is 3 percentage points less than their representation in the total sample.

The likelihood of health insurance coverage and payment through one's work is positively related to wage level. The highest percentage (89) with paid health insurance receive the second highest wage, followed by 82 percent in the highest wage category. On the other hand, 71 percent with the lowest wage receive no health insurance, and over half (56 percent) in the second lowest wage group are also not covered by employer health insurance. Compared to health insurance coverage, an even higher percentage of low wage earners do not have an employer pension plan, and a lower percentage of high wage earners do.

Table 5.6 Percent Distribution[a] of Select Demographic and Employment Characteristics by Wage[e]

Sample Size: 389

	Wage[d]				
	<$3.69	$3.70 - $5.03	$5.04 - $6.62	$6.63 - $9.17	>$9.18
*Age***					
55-61	38	56	62	74	67
62-64	8	13	13	15	14
65-69	22	18	14	9	13
≥70	32	13	11	1	6
*Education***					
Some High School	60	35	37	23	18
High School Grad	26	49	47	46	37
Some College	5	12	14	21	18
College Graduate	5	3	1	4	14
Post-College	5	3	0	5	14
*Occupation***					
Professional/Mgmt	9	5	8	17	40
Tech/Sales/Serv/Adm Sup	73	86	65	63	46
Operators/Fabricators	18	9	28	21	14
*Employer/Union Pd Health Ins***					
NIU/None	71	56	32	12	18
All	17	21	39	45	50
Part	12	23	29	44	32
*Employer Pension Plan***					
No	84	81	58	40	31
Yes	16	19	42	60	69

Source: Author's Tabulation of U.S. Bureau of the Census, Survey of Income and Program Participation (SIPP), Wave IV, 1984.

[a]Percentages may not add up to 100 due to rounding.

[d]Wage divided into five equal quintiles.

[e]Missing observations = 1.5%

***p<.01

Non-Earned Income

Non-earned income is divided into four equal subgroups with values of $665 or less, $666-$3,312, $3,313-$6,619, and $6,620 or more (Table 5.7). The first group represents double the size of the other three groups. Since there is no non-earned income in the first quintile, the lowest two non-earned income categories are collapsed into one.

Table 5.7 Percentiles of Annual Non-Earned Income

Percentiles	Working
20	$ 0
40	665
60	3,312
80	6,619

Source: Author's Tabulation of U.S. Bureau of the Census, Survey of Income and
           Program Participation (SIPP), Wave IV, 1984.
[c]Rounded to nearest dollar.

The relationship of non-earned income with age, marital status, education, occupation, and hours of work is highly significant at $p<.01$ (Table 5.8). The highest percentages of non-earned income are among widows: 68 percent and 72 percent in the higher two categories of non-earned income, (substantially above their 50 percent representation of the sample as a whole). In other words, widows are most likely to have more non-earned income. In contrast, divorced women are most represented at the two lowest non-earnings categories (42 percent and 33 percent respectively). Never married women are relatively equally split among the four non-earnings categories, with the lower two categories at 16 percent and the highest at 13 percent.

Table 5.8 Percent Distribution of Select Demographic and Employment Characteristics by Non-Earned Income[a]

Sample Size: 395

	Non-Earned Income			
	< $665	$666 - $3,312	$3,313- $6,619	> $6,620
*Age***				
55-61	18	80	29	29
62-64	15	10	14	11
65-69	6	9	23	30
≥70	1	1	33	29
*Marital Status***				
Widowed	34	44	68	72
Divorced	42	33	15	11
Separated	7	8	3	4
Never Married	16	16	14	13
*Education***				
Some High School	40	25	47	20
High School Graduate	42	51	35	37
Some College	10	11	9	28
College Graduate	4	5	5	8
Post-College	4	8	4	8
*Occupation***				
Professional/Managerial	13	15	12	25
Tech/Sales/Serv/ Admin Sup	58	69	79	70
Operator/Fabricator	29	16	9	5
*Hours of Work***				
1-17	3	10	31	32
18-34	10	21	35	27
≥35	87	69	35	42

Source: Author's Tabulation of U.S. Bureau of the Census, Survey of Income and Program Participation (SIPP), Wave IV, 1984.

[a]Percentages may not add up to 100 due to rounding.

***p<.01

The fact that widows, even if they are working, have more non-earned income is not surprising, since many of these women have inherited survivor's pension benefits and income-producing assets from their deceased spouses. In contrast, divorced women tend to have the least amount of non-earned income, with 42 percent having no more than $665 in asset income. Divorced and separated women may be more likely to be economically vulnerable with more limited work histories (compared to never married women of their cohort) and with no other source of financial support (compared to their widowed peers).

What does seem surprising related to non-earned income is the fact that the youngest women in this sample, ages 55 to 61, have the least non-earned income. They represent 78 percent and 80 percent of the lower two non-earnings categories, (a great deal higher than their representation at 59 percent in the sample as a whole). Why? The answer may be that in addition to their "younger" older age that makes them more capable of working and better able to find jobs, their motivation to work is improved by the reality that these women have no or little non-earned income as a safety net. Also, it is unlikely that the "younger" women are collecting Social Security or private pension benefits.

Clearly, those with less education, defined as high school or less, represent the largest percentages of non-earners at all income levels, especially the lowest. The largest percentage throughout all levels of education is 51 percent, who are the high school graduates making $666-$3,312 of non-earned income; this subgroup is overrepresented in the sample by 10.5 percent. The next largest group (47 percent) are those with less than high school education with non-earned income of $3,313-$6,619. It would appear that single women with less education are influenced by other confounding variables that affect their non-earned income, primarily their marital status (i.e., whether they are widowed or divorced). However, educated women—with at least some college education—are obviously more represented in the highest non-earnings category: 44 percent, compared to only 24 percent of this education subgroup in the total sample.

The largest occupational group of single older working women with non-earned income is the technical/sales/service/administrative support category making $3,133-$6,619; these women represent 79 percent of the second highest non-earnings category, 12 percent more than this occupational group in the sample as a whole. In fact, this occupational category is overrepresented in the three higher non-earnings groups and only underrepresented in the lowest at 58 percent. Since non-earned income is so heavily influenced by assets from a former spouse (deceased or divorced), occupation, like education, does not stand on its own in determining non-earned income. However, in the highest non-earnings category there is an overrepresentation of professionals/managers, as there are college educated women, which probably speaks to a dual labor market, affecting both non-earned as well as earned income.

As expected, those women working more hours—that is, full time, rather than either category of part time—have the least amount of non-earned income; 87 percent of the women in the lowest non-earnings category work full time, with a drop from 69 percent to 35 percent in the next two higher non-earnings categories, and then an increase to 42 percent in the highest non-earnings category.

In the part-time categories, single older working women are overrepresented in the higher two non-earnings groups: 31 percent and 32 percent in the less-than-half-time category. In the less-than-half-time group, these percentages represent double the overall percentage of this category in the sample at large. In other words, single older women working less than half time represent 16 percent of the total sample and twice that in the two higher non-earnings categories. The women working half time or more are significantly overrepresented at 35 percent and 27 percent in the higher two non-earned income categories but not double. The statistics indicate that there is a strong negative association between non-earned income and labor force participation (hours of work). The more these women have financially, the less likely they are to work half time or more; and the less these women have, the more likely they are to work more hours. Poor health, which could be another explanation for limited labor force participation and resulting reliance upon Supplemental Security Income (SSI) or Social Security, accounts for less than 2 percent of the sample.

Total Annual Income

Total annual income is comprised of total earnings and total non-earnings. The sample is divided into five equal-sized total income categories: ≤$7,939, $7,940-$11,314, $11,315-$14,604, $14,605-$19,853, and >$19,854 (Table 5.9).

Table 5.9 Percentiles of Annual Income[c]

Sample Size: 395

Percentiles	Annual Income
20	$ 7,939
40	11,314
60	14,604
80	19,853

Source: Author's Tabulation of U.S. Bureau of the Census, Survey of Income and Program Participation (SIPP), Wave IV, 1984.
[c]Rounded to nearest dollar.

The research analysis shows no significant relationship between total annual income and age or marital status. There is a strong positive association (p<.01) between total annual income and education, occupation, and working hours, (not shown in Table). Whereas single women with less than a high school diploma earn the least (62 percent of the lowest income category), college-educated women (with at least some college) amount to only 54 percent of the total highest income category. In other words, the less educated women account for more lower incomes than the more educated women account for higher incomes. Also, professionals/managers are more likely to be in the highest income category (42 percent), which equals over half (54 percent) of their total sample number. Women in technical/sales/ service/ administrative support jobs are more spread out among income categories, with the least in the highest subgroup, (only 15 percent of their total sample number). And, blue collar workers are weighted more at the lower end of the income scale, with only 9 percent of this occupational group having income of more than $19,854 annually.

The average annual income (Table 5.1) of those working least (1-17 hours) is approximately half that of those working full time: $9,584 compared to $18,356. Two-thirds of the average total income of those working the least is attributed to non-earned income ($6,440), whereas only 16 percent ($2,956) of full-time workers' average total income comes from non-earnings. In other words, single older women working full time rely primarily on their earnings as the basis of their total annual income, less-than-half-time workers rely least on earnings for financial "survival," and more-than-half-time workers count on an almost even split between earnings (53 percent) and non-earnings (47 percent) for their total annual income ($10,536 on average).

Household Wealth

Household wealth (or total net worth) is defined as the value of total assets minus debts. It is a measure of how income has exceeded needs over the life cycle. For most older people, home ownership provides the basis for most of their amassed wealth over time. And, while home ownership has not been investigated as part of this research study, overall wealth has. It can be assumed that the single older women with low incomes also have low asset holdings, so that assets do little to raise their incomes (Crown, Mutschler, Schulz, and Loew, 1993).

For purposes of analysis, the sample is divided into five equal-sized wealth categories: <$7,671, $7,672-$30,405, $30,406-$58,309, $58,310-$86,758, and >$86,759 (Table 5.10). According to the research findings, wealth is not related with any statistical significance to age, employer provided health insurance, or hours of work (Table 5.11). Interestingly, wealth is strongly associated (p<.01) with marital status, education, employer provided pension plan, average annual earnings and non-earnings, and average annual income. And, wealth is less strongly (p<.05) related to occupation.

Table 5.10 Percentiles of Household Wealth (Total Net Worth)[c]

Sample Size: 395

Percentiles	Total Net Worth
20	$ 7,671
40	30,405
60	58,309
80	86,758

Source: Author's Tabulation of U.S. Bureau of the Census, Survey of Income and Program Participation (SIPP), Wave IV, 1984.
[c]Rounded to nearest dollar.

Widows have the highest representation in the second wealthiest net worth category, with 61 percent having at least $58,310. In contrast, in the other three marital status groups (divorced, separated, and never married), the highest percentages are in the lowest net worth categories with less than $7,671: 41 percent, 10 percent, and 20 percent respectively. It appears that widows, with the benefit of assets of their deceased husbands, are least vulnerable financially and that separated

Table 5.11 Percent Distribution[a] of Select Demographic and Employment Characteristics by Wealth[c]

Sample Size: 395

	Wealth[d]				
	< $7,671	$7,672 - $30,405	$30,406 - $58,309	$58,310 - $86,758	>$86,759
Age					
55-61	63	65	59	49	59
62-64	15	8	18	14	10
65-69	10	15	14	15	20
≥70	11	13	9	22	10
Marital Status*					
Widowed	29	51	53	61	58
Divorced	41	33	29	20	22
Separated	10	6	6	3	3
Never Married	20	10	11	16	18
Education*					
Some High School	53	38	43	27	11
High School Graduate	29	48	39	48	43
Some College	8	9	15	10	27
College Graduate	4	3	3	8	9
Post-College	6	3		8	10
Hours of Work					
1-17	16	14	14	20	14
18-34	18	24	20	22	19
≥35	66	62	66	58	67
Occupation**					
Professional/Mgmt	10	10	13	18	27
Tech/Sales/Serv/Adm Sup	65	71	66	67	66
Operator/Fabricator	25	19	22	15	8
Employer/Union Pd Hlth Ins					
NIU	42	39	43	42	24
All	27	34	34	29	47
Part	32	27	23	29	29
Employer Pension Plan*					
No	68	68	57	61	42
Yes	32	32	43	39	58

Source: Author's Tabulation of U.S. Bureau of the Census, Survey of Income and Program Participation (SIPP), Wave IV, 1984.

[a]Percentages may not add up to 100 due to rounding.

[c]Rounded to nearest dollar.

[d]Wealth divided into five equal quintiles.

***P<.01

** p<.05

women, although they are fewest in number in the sample, are most vulnerable (Loew, 1992). Also, widows, like married couples, are more likely to own homes that are included in their asset holdings.

More education corresponds clearly to more wealth; 19 percent of the sample with at least a college degree have over $86,759 in total net worth (with an additional 27 percent with some college education), as compared to only 11 percent of those with less than high school education in the highest wealth category.

One-quarter of the white collar women have the most wealth, compared to two-thirds of the pink collar and only 8 percent of the blue collar having the most net worth. Pink collar workers are somewhat evenly dispersed throughout the wealth categories, blue collar more represented in the lower wealth categories, and white collar in the higher wealth categories.

Wealth and annual income are strongly related at the p<.01 (Table 5.12). In the two highest income categories, those with more wealth comprise the larger percent of each income group. The largest overall percentage (39 percent) lies with the single working women with both the highest income and the most wealth. Of course, this finding is not surprising, since amassed wealth over the life cycle is primarily related to saved annual income used to purchase homes and other assets. The next highest percentage are women from the same sample with the least amount of both income and wealth. If annual income is so strongly associated in the positive direction with household wealth, then this data may suggest a rationale for means-tested public programs and support for the elderly who have neither wealth nor income.

Although the research variable that relates to pensions offers information only about provision of employer pensions, not amount of benefits, there is a strong positive association (p <.01) between access to these pensions and total wealth. Single older working women with pensions established by their employers are most likely to have more wealth than those without pensions. As access to retirement plans increase, so does wealth: from a low of 32 percent to a high of 58 percent.

Table 5.12 Percent Distribution of Household Wealth by Annual Income[a]***

Sample Size: 395

	Annual Income[d]				
	<$7,939	$7,940-$11,314	$11,31-$14,604	$14,60-$19,853	>$19,854
Wealth					
≤ $7,671	37	18	27	10	9
$7,672 - $30,405	23	25	23	18	11
$30,406 - $58,309	19	29	16	19	16
$58,310 - $86,758	18	16	16	25	24
≥ $86,759	4	11	18	28	39
Total Number	79	79	79	79	79

Source: Author's Tabulation of U.S. Bureau of the Census, Survey of Income and Program Participation (SIPP), Wave IV, 1984.

[a]Percentages may not add up to 100 due to rounding.
[d]Annual Income divided into five equal quintiles.
***p<.01

SUMMARY OF FINDINGS: INCOME AND WEALTH VARIABLES

For the purpose of this study, five income variables are explored: annual earnings, hourly wage, annual non-earnings, total annual income, and household wealth. Working hours, whether single older women are working full time or part time, are strongly associated (p<.01) with all but household wealth. If these women work full time, they are more likely to have higher earnings, higher wages, and higher total incomes. Annual earnings account for 84 percent of the total income of full-time workers, reduced to 53 percent for more-than-half-time workers and only 33 percent for less-than-half-time workers. However, there is a strong negative association between working hours and non-earned income: full-time workers have the least.

One of the more interesting findings is the variation in hourly wage among the three categories of working hours. In 1984, full-time single older working women are making the most, $7.66 on average per hour. However, the women making the least wages are not the less-than-half-time workers. The 18-34 hour per week workers make 71 cents less than the workers with the least hours and $3.11 less than full timers. Because of substantially reduced wages among 18-34 hour workers, it follows that their total earnings are less than twice that of 1-17 hour workers. In fact, combining earnings with non-earned income, the less than half-time workers have 91 percent of the total income of the more than half-time workers and just over one half that of full-time workers. It is unclear if more-than-half-time workers who earn less hourly represent a different occupational mix or if they are motivated for benefits other than money (e.g., access to health insurance and/or pensions, job satisfaction, or social supports).

As expected, taking into consideration dual labor market theory, single older women with more education (at least some college) and higher status jobs (professionals or managers) are much more likely (p<.01) to have higher earnings, hourly wages, non-earned income, and total income. Occupation is somewhat less strongly associated with household wealth (p<.05).

Age is strongly associated with some income variables and not with others. Clearly, the younger single older women workers (55-61 years old) are more apt to receive higher earnings and wages, but have the least non-earned income. This finding suggests that these younger single women are more financially dependent on their jobs. And, contrary to what one might expect, age has no association with total income or household wealth. In other words, older single women, on average, do not have more income or wealth nor do younger single women have less.

Marital status is the other demographic variable that presents a mixed picture related to economic well being. Although there is no association between marital status and hourly wage, or total income, marital status is related to earnings (p<.05) and, even more so, to non-earned income and household wealth (p<.01). Compared to their percentages in the overall sample, widows are clustered at the lower end of the earnings scale, divorcees at the upper end, and separated and never married in the middle. On the other hand, widows fair better than every other category of singlehood regarding household wealth.

Employer or union paid health insurance and retirement plan coverage are also positively associated with higher earnings and wages as well as with household wealth. The relationship between pension coverage and both earnings and wages is relatively obvious, since other variables, such as working hours, affect pension availability as well as higher earnings and wages. However, *access* to an employer pension plan, not yet available or having measurable worth, implies nothing by itself about current wealth. It is, therefore, interesting that pensions are a barometer of wealth, even if not yet an actual contributor.

Small private companies of less than 25 employees offer the most part-time jobs, but at tremendous cost to single older women who, on average, earn much less than equivalent women who work in large sites (over 100 employees). The best case scenarios for highest earnings are large work sites in private companies.

ANALYSIS OF VARIANCE

The four ANOVAs discussed in this chapter are related to factors affecting the economic well being of working and non-working single older women. The first three focus on the working women and include important demographic, employment, and income variables. Hours of work is considered in the ANOVAs of the working women as one of many independent variables that have an effect on three income aggregates: mean total annual earnings, non-earned income, and overall income. The fourth ANOVA related to non-working women includes significant demographic variables, (specifically age, marital status, education, and living arrangements), and one important income variable (household wealth). Discussion of the fourth ANOVA follows in the section comparing non-working with working women.

Mean Total Annual Earnings Income

Earnings have a high overall level of statistical association (p <.01) with working hours, marital status, age, education, occupation, employer provided health insurance and pensions, work site size, hourly wage, and household wealth (Table 5.13). In the ANOVA of mean total annual earnings, the average annual earnings differ at the p<.01 level by working hours, education, and hourly wage, at the p<.05 level by occupation and employer provided pension plan, and at the p<.10 level by employer provided health insurance. None of these associations are surprising. As expected, hours of work, hourly wage and level of education have significant bearing on single older working women's total earnings. Education is more significant than occupation on annual earnings; in other words, level of education is more strongly associated with earnings for single older women than the kind of jobs they hold. This finding is in contrast to the experience of many men who make more money even with less education (e.g., skilled tradesmen with no college education).

Of all the variables with a significant effect on total annual earnings, employer paid health insurance is associated the least. Although access to health insurance on the job seems to strongly affect working hours, it has much less bearing on annual earnings, particularly as compared to other significant variables in the analysis of variance.

Table 5.13 ANOVA of Mean Total Annual Earnings: Working Women

Source of Variation[b]	F-Statistic	Significance
Weekly Work Hours	37.191	.000***
Marital Status	.309	.819
Age	.623	.600
Education	4.604	.001***
Occupation	4.139	.017**
Employer/Union Pd Hlth Ins	2.945	.054*
Work Site Size	.936	.393
Employer Pension Plan	4.135	.043**
Hourly Wage	65.271	.000***
Household Wealth	.407	.804
Total Explained Variation	*37.399*	*.000***

Source: Author's Tabulation of U.S. Bureau of the Census, Survey of Income and Program Participation (SIPP), Wave IV, 1984.

[b]Except for education, only the explanatory variables that demonstrate statistic significance in chi squares are included in the ANOVA.
***p<.01
** p<.05
* p<.10

Mean Total Annual Non-Earned Income

Although only one variable demonstrates some significance in this analysis of variance, the relationship between non-earned income and the same variables used in the previous analysis of variance in terms of total explained variation is equally strong at the p<.01 level (Table 5.14). When controlling for these variables, only household wealth has significance at the p<.10 level. This finding is expected, since wealth is substantially related to income from all sources, including non-earnings. A major source of non-earnings is asset income, which is directly related to the size of asset holdings.

Table 5.14 ANOVA of Mean Total Annual Non-Earned Income: Working Women

Source of Variation[b]	F-Statistic	Significance
Weekly Work Hours	1.803	.166
Marital Status	1.981	.117
Age	1.857	.137
Education	1.397	.235
Occupation	1.151	.317
Employer/Union Pd Hlth Ins	.208	.812
Work Site Size	.821	.441
Employer Pension Plan	1.726	.190
Hourly Wage	.73	.591
Household Wealth	2.313	.057*
Total Explained Variation	*2.764*	*.000****

Source: Author's Tabulation of U.S. Bureau of the Census, Survey of Income and
          Program Participation (SIPP), Wave IV, 1984.

[b]Except for education, only the explanatory variables that demonstrate statistic
    significance in chi squares are included in the ANOVA.
***p<.01
*   p<.10

Mean Total Annual Income

Table 5.15 shows that average income differs at the p<.01 level by hours of work per week, education, and hourly wage, at the p<.05 level by occupation and household wealth, and at the p<.10 level by age. The other categorical variables, when considered altogether, have no statistical significance on mean total annual income.

Intuitively, it makes sense that annual income is strongly related to weekly work hours and to hourly wage, given that most of the income of these single older working women is derived from earnings. Studies have shown repeatedly that women's education and occupations do not correspond as well to their total income as do men's. One might assume an even greater discrepancy with an older population where women experience more academic and employment constraints. However, the research findings demonstrate the importance of education and, to a lesser degree, occupation on single older women's income level.

Table 5.15 ANOVA of Mean Total Annual Income: Working Women

Source of Variation[b]	F-Statistic	Significance
Weekly Work Hours	6.822	.001***
Marital Status	1.567	.197
Age	2.102	.100*
Education	4.502	.001***
Occupation	3.915	.021**
Employer/Union Pd Hlth Ins	.935	.394
Work Site Size	1.797	.167
Employer Pension Plan	.017	.895
Hourly Wage	22.520	.000***
Household Wealth	2.536	.040**
Total Explained Variation	*14.564*	*.000****

Source: Author's Tabulation of U.S. Bureau of the Census, Survey of Income and Program Participation (SIPP), Wave IV, 1984.

[b]Except for education, only the explanatory variables that demonstrate statistic significance in chi squares are included in the ANOVA.

***$p<.01$
** $p<.05$
* $p<.10$

One would expect that the sources of variation with mean total annual income would be a mix of the results of single older women's earnings and non-earned income (e.g., household wealth) results. The findings support the fact that they are.

ECONOMIC COMPARISON: NON-WORKING VERSUS WORKING WOMEN

In some ways, the non-working sample looks similar to the working sample of single older women. Level of education is a significant source of variation in mean total annual income for both working and non-working women. Marital status for both groups is not significant when controlling for other variables. On the other hand, the variables of age and household wealth are associated more strongly with the average annual income of non-working more than working women.

Mean Total Annual Income: Non-Working Women

Because so many variables, determined to be significant through chi-squares, are related to employment which is obviously not relevant to non-working women, half the number of variables are included in the non-working women's ANOVA: age, marital status, education, living arrangements, and household wealth (Table 5.16). All the variables except for marital status significantly explain (p<.01) the variation of mean total annual income. Clearly, household wealth is related to mean total annual income for both working and non-working single older women, yet more significantly for non-working (p<.01). In terms of demographic variables, older, less educated single women who live alone are more likely to have low total annual incomes. In addition to the individual sources of variation, the explained overall variation is highly significant (p<.01).

Table 5.16 ANOVA of Mean Total Annual Income[f]: Non-Working Women

Source of Variation[b]	F-Statistic	Significance
Marital Status	.533	.659
Age	3.901	.009***
Education	21.573	.000***
Living Arrangements	64.170	.000***
Household Wealth	174.653	.000***
Total Explained Variation	72.237	.000***

Source: Author's Tabulation of U.S. Bureau of the Census, Survey of Income and
          Program Participation (SIPP), Wave IV, 1984.

[b]Except for education, only the explanatory variables that demonstrate statistic
significance in chi squares are included in the ANOVA.

[f]Total annual income = total annual non-earned income for non-working women.
***p<.01

Although marital status is highly significant (p <.01) in a dichotomous comparison between working and non-working single older women (Table 4.11), it is the only variable that shows no significance in the analysis of variance of total annual income of non-working women. In other words, when controlling for all the variables that demonstrate most significance among the non-working sample, marital status (e.g., widowhood) cannot explain total annual income with the same degree of certainty as it is able to explain the likelihood of working.

Values and Sources of Income: Working versus Non-Working Women

Both groups are either very poor or very rich. The buffer against economic hardship, if not poverty, for the working women are their earnings. According to the four primary percentiles of household total net worth (Table 5.17) for both non-working and working women, there is a substantial spread between the very poor and the very rich. In the middle ranges (40th and 60th percentiles), working makes more of a difference in household total net worth than not working. Yet, at either extreme, worth is much lower (almost nothing), due to many with negative income that pulls down the average, and much higher (over $100,000) among the non-working sample. Overall household total net worth on average does not vary substantially between women working and not working; working women have approximately 10 percent more in household asset holdings than non-working women (Table 5.18).

Annual income, which is derived from earnings plus property, transfer and other miscellaneous sources, reflects the positive value of working for all percentiles (Table 5.19), not just the middle ranges as noted with household total net worth. In fact, workers rely on more than two times more income per year than non-workers. However, workers in the 80th percentile are still making less than $20,000 a year, only about $12,000 more than those in the 20th percentile. With very little in the way of non-earned income, working women count on their earnings to protect them from poverty. On average 77 percent of single older working women's income is derived from their earnings, in contrast to an almost equal percentage (73 percent) of income among non-working women derived from "other" sources, primarily public and private pensions (Table 5.20).

Table 5.17 Comparative Percentiles for Household Total Net Worth of Working and Non-Working Women[c]

Sample Size: 395

Percentiles	Working	Non-Working
20	$ 7,671	$ 41
40	30,405	20,096
60	58,309	53,010
80	86,758	101,868

Source: Author's Tabulation of U.S. Bureau of the Census, Survey of Income and Program Participation (SIPP), Wave IV, 1984.
[c]Rounded to nearest dollar.

Table 5.18 Comparative Income Sources and Household Asset Holdings[c] of Working and Non-Working Women

Sample Sizes	(n=395)	(n=2,166)
Sources & Holdings	Working	Non-Working
Household Total Net Worth	$ 67,324	$ 60,816
Mean Monthly Income Sources	1,281	611
Earnings	980	0
Property	93	140
Transfer	4	26
Other	206	444
Median Total Monthly Income	1070	469

Source: Author's Tabulation of U.S. Bureau of the Census, Survey of Income and Program Participation (SIPP), Wave IV, 1984.
[c]Rounded to nearest dollar.

Table 5.19 Comparative Annual Income^c of Working and Non-Working Women by Percentiles

Sample Sizes	(n=395)	(n=2,166)
Percentiles	Working	Non-Working
20	$ 7,939	$ 3,540
40	11,314	4,740
60	14,604	6,540
80	19,853	10,620

Source: Author's Tabulation of U.S. Bureau of the Census, Survey of Income and Program Participation (SIPP), Wave IV, 1984.
^cRounded to nearest dollar.

Table 5.20 Comparative Percent Distribution of Mean Monthly Income by Source for Working and Non-Working Women

Sample Sizes	(n=395)	(n=2,166)
	Working	Non-Working
Source		
Earnings	77	0
Property	7	23
Transfer	0	4
Other	16	73

Source: Author's Tabulation of U.S. Bureau of the Census, Survey of Income and Program Participation (SIPP), Wave IV, 1984.

Although working women certainly rely on their earnings as a buffer against financial desperation, using the average rather than the mean inflates somewhat the economic security of both the single women workers and the non-workers. The mean takes into account outliers who tend to skew the experience of the greater number, whereas the median represents the middle of the sample. The median total monthly income for working women is approximately $200 less (84 percent of the mean) and for non-working women, $140 less (77 percent of the mean), as shown in Table 5.18.

Because of the unexpected finding related to high labor force participation of single women 70 years of age and older, income characteristics of both working (Table 5.21) and non-working (not in

Single Older Women in the Workforce

Table 5.21 Percent Distribution of Income Characteristics by Age: Working Women[a]

Sample Size: 395

	(n=254)	(n=51)	(n=59)	(n=51)
	Age			
	55-61	62-64	65-69	> 70
Hourly Wage***				
≤ $ 3.69	13	12	29	50
$3.70-$5.03	19	20	24	20
$5.04-$6.62	21	20	19	18
$6.63-$9.17	25	24	12	2
≥$ 9.18	23	22	17	10
Annual Earnings Income***				
≤ $3,600	8	20	34	65
$3,601-$7,560	18	14	37	16
$7,561-$12,000	26	25	8	10
$12,001-$17,530	24	18	7	6
≥ $17,531	24	24	14	4
Annual NonEarned Income***				
≤ $ 665	53	45	17	2
$666-$3,312	27	16	12	2
$3,313-$6,619	10	22	31	51
≥$ 6,620	10	18	41	45
Total Annual Income				
≤ $ 7,939	18	12	22	37
$7,940-$11,314	19	24	22	20
$11,315-$14,604	20	25	22	14
$14,605-$19,853	20	20	20	20
≥$ 19,854	24	20	14	10
Household Wealth				
≤$ 7,671	21	24	14	18
$7,672-$30,405	22	12	20	20
$30,406-$58,309	20	27	19	14
$58,310-$86,758	17	22	20	33
≥ $ 86,759	20	16	27	16

Source: Author's Tabulation of U.S. Bureau of the Census, Survey of Income and
Program Participation (SIPP), Wave IV, 1984.

[a]Percentages may not add up to 100 due to rounding.
***p<.01

Table) women are analyzed by age so as to understand more clearly the financial profiles of these women 70+ who remain in the workforce. It is interesting to note that hourly wage, annual earnings income, and annual non-earned income differ significantly by age (p<.01) among working women. Among the oldest workers (≥70 years of age), half make the lowest wage, representing 31 percent more than the lowest wage earners in the 65-69 year old age category. Another 20 percent of the oldest workers make the second lowest wage. It follows, also, that their earnings are significantly the least: 65 percent of those ≥70 years old make ≤$3,600. Their non-earned income, on the other hand, is clustered in the two higher ranges. The substantial percentage increase in non-earned income from 62-64 to 65-69 years of age probably represents receipt of Social Security and private pensions.

Although employment-related income variables and non-earned income are highly associated with age for single older working women, total annual income and household wealth are not. Nor are these latter two income characteristics associated with the age of non-working single older women (not in Table). The explanation of no significance between age and total annual income for working women may be that earnings income and non-earned income operate in opposite directions so that they basically cancel each other out in terms of total income. Among the oldest women, the workers are substantially clustered in the lowest income categories, whereas the non-workers are spread relatively equally among all five income categories. However, it should be noted that 80 percent of the working sample have more than twice the total income of the non-working women. Thus, the critical distinction between the economic status of the working versus non-working single oldest women is the earnings income.

Household wealth is fairly evenly spread out among wealth categories and ages for both working and non-working single older women. However, the youngest non-working women have the largest representation (37 percent) with the least wealth (not in Table), and the oldest workers in the second highest wealth category have the largest representation (33 percent) with the most wealth. It is curious as to why so many single women without back-up wealth or access to Social Security do not work. Do they have limited education or occupational skills which make jobs hard to find or least interesting to maintain? And, why are the oldest workers with household wealth between $58,310 and $86,758 continuing to work? If their wealth is essentially non-liquid and in the form of home ownership, they still may feel a financial need to work. Or, even with low wages and earnings, they may enjoy their jobs and/or the social contacts from working.

Non-working women tend to be either very rich or very poor. However, even those in the middle wealth categories who appear quite economically comfortable may be "house poor," since home ownership is the primary contributor to household wealth. And, additionally, total annual incomes among these non-working women, even inclusive of Social Security and private pension benefits, are, on average, still quite low.

SUMMARY OF FINDINGS: INCOME-RELATED ANOVAS AND COMPARISION BETWEEN WORKING ANDNON-WORKING WOMEN

The ANOVA of mean total annual earnings indicates the importance of weekly work hours, education, and hourly wage on the earnings of single older working women: more working hours, education, and hourly wage are strongly associated with higher earnings. To a lesser degree, occupation and employer pension plans, followed by employer paid health insurance, are associated with earnings. The ANOVA of mean total annual non-earned income is only related with any significance to household wealth and not to any other demographic or economic variables in the analysis. This makes sense as different forms of wealth (e.g., rental property, stocks, and bonds) often generate non-earned income.

The ANOVA of mean total annual income is strongly associated with weekly work hours, education, and hourly wage: the more hours that single older women work, the more advanced their education and the greater their wages, the more likely they are to have better total incomes. Occupations and household wealth contribute to a lesser degree and age to the least significant degree to annual income.

Economic well being among single older women is certainly influenced by working and the resulting earnings income. On average,single older working women live on at least twice as much income monthly and annually as non-working single older women. Their average household total net worth is approximately 10 percent more than that of their non-working counterparts. Yet, because earnings are the primary source of their income, which accounts for over three-quarters of their total income, not working—even with income replacement from Social Security and possible employer pensions—could cause not only a sudden drop in their standard of living but also economic distress. These working women do not have the same non-earned income or amassed wealth as wealthier non-working women. Therefore, without earned income they are more likely to become part of the non-working poor. It is interesting to note that the oldest women in the sample, representing 12 percent of the total, continue to work, although they receive Social Security benefits (which are quite meager at less than $5,000 annually) and although they make significantly low wages and earnings. It is unclear as to whether these women work for the added income, regardless of how limited, or for the satisfaction gained from their jobs.

Surely, earnings are important for the survival—economic and psychological—of many single older women. However, earnings are not the panacea for all these women, particularly as they age and jobs become increasingly scarce. The "carrot" to work must be made available through a variety of channels (e.g., a range of job opportunities, including varying hours of work), yet there has to be financial security of other kinds when working is no longer an option. Chapter 6 will explore these options.

Chapter VI

Policy Implications

INTRODUCTION

As the SIPP research demonstrates, single older women, even many widows, do not have adequate income. They are primarily in low-paying, unskilled jobs, often with no retirement benefits and with access to employer paid health insurance only if they work full time. Part-time workers, mostly older and widowed, are at even more risk for low earnings and low total incomes. The SIPP data set does not ask older women why they work. Nonetheless, it is reasonable to conclude from their meager income that many single older women (ages 55 and older) work because they have to more than because they want to. Those who work because they want to are more likely to be skilled with at least some college education.

If earnings are the best buffer against economic hardship, if not poverty, for single older women, should society force them to keep working even though married older women and single or married older men are not faced with the same "choice?" And, do these single older women really have a choice, when the alternative to working for many of them is living in poverty? The choice not to work, available mostly to men, is based upon the adequacy of their Social Security and private pension benefits as well as their assets upon retirement. Unlike many men, most working women, particularly of this older cohort, have meager Social Security (Golden, 1987; Fierst, 1990)—less than $5,000 for every single older woman in the research sample (1984)—and little or no access to employer-provided pension plans (Binstock, 1985). Unlike most men, these single working women from this study have on average little non-earnings income and, therefore, rely almost exclusively on their earnings for economic survival.

The issue of economic equity has become fiercely disputed in the public arena, but the argument of equity is generally couched in terms of generations (Chakravarty and Weisman, 1988; Kingson, Hirshhorn, and Cornman, 1986; Kotlikoff, 1993; Longman, 1985) rather than gender or marital status. The common cry nowadays is that children more than elders are more likely to be poor and, in times of scarce resources, government should set aside money for the young more than the old. The public issue of scarce resources and intergenerational inequity includes the argument for health care rationing: life-saving care must be limited solely based upon a patient's age (Binstock, and Post, 1991). What this narrowly defined political position is ignoring is the economic and physical inequities among subgroups of elders, specifically single older women.

Given the multiple obstacles in the way of single older women, one solution to their economic vulnerability is the "stick"—that is, requiring them to work until they are no longer able physically or mentally to do so. The "stick" approach to keeping these women in the workforce might include punitive disincentives to stop working, such as decreasing or taxing Social Security benefits at all levels, reducing private pension benefits, increasing the eligibility age for Social Security, and raising the actuarial penalty for early retirement. The "stick" approach might also be the requirement (for economic survival) of regular full-time work without the choice of alternative work schedules. However, without the "carrots" that offer these women positive incentives to continue working or the choice to work less or not at all, (as men often choose to do), some single older women will remain trapped in the labor force.

The remainder of this chapter will present recommendations for policy reforms that respond more to the "carrot" than the "stick" approach. The initial policy recommendations are closely related to the findings of this study. The more general recommendations that follow, divided into sections on employment, income adequacy, caregiving, and health care reforms, highlight some real opportunities for employment choice and for financial well being above the poverty line.

POLICY RECOMMENDATIONS RELATED TO RESEARCH FINDINGS

Who are the single older women most at risk for living in poverty? What government legislation and employment policies need to be established for the protection of these women? And, what is the intent of these policies: to provide incentives for working (in order to raise women's income levels and thereby lower society's economic responsibility), or to offer a real choice of working or not working with a baseline of income adequacy in either instance?

Based upon the findings of this research, there are specific recommendations of policy reforms for single older women that respond to their unique economic risks. Some demographic, employment, and income characteristics more than others account for the financial vulnerability of single older working women. According to this study, low wage and salary earners are often older than 62, widowed, with less than a high school diploma, with no employer-provided health insurance or pension plan, and working part time in small, privately owned sites. Surprisingly the lowest wage earners are more likely to work more than half time rather than less than half time; they make on average 71 cents (or 13 percent) less than those working the least number of hours.

Because only 16 percent of earners' total income on average is comprised of non-earned income, we can assume that many of those with the lowest wages and salary levels are at economic risk. In other words, most of these earners do not have sufficient non-earned income to augment their total annual income and, therefore, rely heavily on their earnings for economic survival. This is particularly true for earners under age 62, who are not eligible for Social Security, which serves the purpose of replacing, at least in part, earnings income. Although there is no way of determining from this research data the amount of replacement income from Social Security, the comparison with non-working women, who live primarily on less than half the annual income of their working counterparts, suggests that income from Social Security alone would substantially lower their standard of living and possibly heighten their vulnerability to poverty.

Hours of work, the primary dependent variable of this study, is positively associated with the economic well being of single older working women. The reasons for this association are not only because full-time work is highly correlated with more income but also because full-time work is significantly related to more job skills, more employee benefits, higher education and larger work site size. The converse is also true: part-time work is strongly associated with less income (and smaller wages), less skilled jobs, fewer or no employee benefits, less education, and smaller work sites.

First and foremost, full-time equivalent wages for part-time workers are an important means of both treating all workers equitably and encouraging their labor force participation. Lower part-time wages, particularly if they tend to adversely impact some classes of workers more than others (e.g., women, minorities, and elders), can be considered discriminatory and illegal. More positively stated, a diverse work force makes fuller use of human capital potential as well as reduces the costs to society of increasing unemployment and retirement. Because a growing percentage of part-time jobs have no permanency or inclusion of benefits, it could be argued that the policy recommendation might even be *more than* full-time equivalent wages for part-time jobs, which would only partially offset the enormous business savings from utilizing contingent workers.

In the same way that a federally legislated minimum wage was established to protect those workers most likely to be economically abused by employers, a federal mandate regarding full-time equivalent wages could assure that all workers of "comparable worth," not based on hours of work, are paid equally. Otherwise, the trend increasingly will be to hire temporary, part-time workers with no job security and making lower wages. This trend serves the needs of employers at the expense of most employees; it accentuates primary and secondary labor markets, in which skilled and educated workers fare well and all others become part of a growing underclass (Shao, 1994, p. 18).

The findings in this study also demonstrate clearly that there is a strong positive relationship between both hours of work and working per se and education; in other words, college-educated women, with at least some college, are more likely to work full time and to stay in the labor force. Education contributes not only to more skilled jobs, (highlighted in this research), but also to increased job satisfaction, (implied but not determined by this study, yet demonstrated by the Onyx/Benton study). If employers' and society's intent is to keep older women in the workforce, incentives related to upgrading job skills must be provided. Job training programs, such as computer courses, offer these workers opportunities to learn new employment skills and keep abreast of current job technology. Training, like education, offers possibilities of new job responsibilities and increased pay as well as enhanced job satisfaction. However, because these training programs are costly and sometimes perceived as risky (with no guaranteed "pay back"), government needs to either support these programs directly (through grants directed to training and job placement programs) or indirectly (through tax credits or deductions to businesses offering on-site training and jobs), which are targeted specifically to low-income elders, who are often identified as single older women. The Targeted Job Tax Credit (TJTC) of the 1993 Omnibus Budget Reconciliation Act (OBRA) begins to address this issue by offering to businesses a one-year 40 percent credit on the first $6,000 of qualified wages for each new economically disadvantaged hiree, many of whom are single older women. (Refer to the section on Employment Reforms that follows for more details on federally funded job training and placement program.)

In addition to full-time equivalent wages and job training programs, another policy recommendation specifically targeted to part-time workers is equal access to health insurance, especially for those under 65 who are not eligible for Medicare. In this study, 35 percent of those under 65 have no health insurance provided and paid for by their employer or union. This finding means that over one-third of the working sample of single older women are uninsured at work. Unlike married women, they have no possibility of coverage by a spouse. Equal access to health care for all persons (both workers and non-workers, part timers and full timers, and those under 65 and those over 65) is a basic human right. And, presently, the cost of non-coverage is borne unfairly by some groups more than others (e.g., hospitals and tax payers more than many businesses that employ increasing numbers of uninsured part-time workers). Health care reform is described more fully in the following section that addresses more generic health policy recommendations.

Pension coverage is the other significant employee benefit that offers a floor of protection to workers who are preparing for retirement (Iams, 1986a). Only 41 percent of all workers in this study have pension coverage, and of those more than three-quarters of part timers are not covered. The data demonstrates a strong negative relationship between pensions and age: "older" single older working women are less likely to have pension coverage. This finding suggests that older workers (beyond 62 or 65) without retirement plans other than Social Security may be trapped in the labor force because of no economic security with retirement.

Access to basic retirement benefits, like health care, is an inalienable right, not a privilege. And, as with health insurance coverage, retirement coverage is a responsibility of both the employer and the government. As more and more employers hire temporary part-time workers, even if they work in a company that offers pension coverage to employees working at least 1,000 hours per year according to ERISA regulations, more firms are substantially reducing their pension costs. Rarely do temporary placement firms offer either pension plans or health insurance coverage to their employees. However, MacTemps Inc., a successful Cambridge-based computer specialist temp agency, is forging a new path for its employees and setting a new standard in the temp marketplace. After logging 1,000 hours within one year, a worker is eligible for a 401K pension plan with a 25 percent company match. MacTemps' business position is that offering benefits attracts and retains good employees, which both lower turnover and recruitment costs as well as appeal to corporate clients who do not want to create "second-class" temporary workers (Shao, 1994, p.18).

Given that only 16 percent of this study sample work less than half time, which amounts to fewer than the 1,000 yearly hours required for ERISA mandated eligibility for pension coverage, it seems that lowering the ERISA required minimum hours would have little effect on access to employer provided pension plans. What may have more effect on the employment of older workers are government incentives to companies offering pension plans, such as business tax deductions or tax credits. Even among the full-time workers in this study, just over half have a retirement plan at work.

If the goal of society is to maintain older workers in the labor force—in response to either a predicted labor shortage or to mounting social costs from an increasing aging population, work incentives need to be geared to both the employer and the employee. Otherwise, society has a responsibility to raise the floor of Social Security for those most at economic risk. It appears from this research study that the oldest single women workers (70+) earning the least are primarily widowed and living alone. However, widows have the most non-earned income, primarily from Social Security after age 65, whereas divorced women have the least. As a result, divorced women may be most at risk financially in retirement, when they rely solely on their non-earned income, essentially their Social Security benefits. If their Social Security were based upon their combined earnings history of their spouses and themselves while they were married or on half of their ex-spouse's Social Security at age 62 with no minimum marital length of time for eligibility (rather than the 10 year requirement that currently exists), divorced women, like widows, would be able to count on a more adequate floor of protection in retirement. For more information on calculating Social Security through earnings sharing, refer to the section that follows on Income Adequacy Reforms.

EMPLOYMENT REFORMS

One of the most significant findings in this research analysis is the fact that most single older women in the labor force are working full time, including one-quarter of those employed beyond age 70. Many of these women are not in the labor force full time because they love their jobs and are well paid. Rather, many stay employed 35 hours a week or more because they need money, access to and payment of health insurance benefits, and eligibility for private pension benefits at retirement. It is interesting to note that the research survey asks about the involuntary nature of part-time work only. It is worth speculating how many full timers among single older women are involuntary or would be involuntary if they were given a real choice of equitable, desirable part-time jobs.

As eager as many of these women may be to keep working, employers may eventually be just as desperate to hold on to older women. Following the baby boomers now entering middle age, some forecasts see a declining number (both relatively and absolutely) of young workers in the labor force as well as rapid growth in industries that are major employers of older people (Fullerton, 1985; Su, 1985; and Work in America Institute, 1980). Between 1986 and 2000 the Commerce Department has projected a negative growth of youth under age 35 (-13.6% for 25-34 year olds) in contrast to a positive growth of 19.6% for those 65 and older and 63.1% for 45-54 year olds. And, by the year 2000 women will comprise almost half of the workforce and two-thirds of the anticipated net labor force growth. Hence, some say that it is crucial—a business necessity—that employers consider ways of making the best use of their labor potential. In fact, the 1983 Social Security Amendments, specifically raising the Social Security normal retirement age to 67 over the period of 2000 to 2027 and after 2027 increasing the actuarial reduction for those electing to take early retirement benefits between ages 62 and 67, is a significant policy change based upon concerns about future labor force shortages and pension financing.

On the other hand, many researchers do not anticipate a rising demand for older workers in the future. One argument is that the projected increase in the size of the middle-aged work force may offset shortages of young workers, ages 16 through 24 (Morrison, 1983). Also, there are predictions that technological change has produced a substitution of physical capital for human capital, resulting in labor surpluses and unemployment (Leontief, 1983).

Whether or not there are labor shortages or labor surpluses, there are entrenched beliefs about older workers that contribute to widely practiced job discrimination (Golden, 1987; Schulz, 1992), resulting lack of access to jobs, and long-term discouragement leading to chronic unemployment. This phenomenon is particularly present during an economic recession when every individual and every category of worker (such as older workers) compete for a shrinking number of jobs and when maintaining or finding jobs among older workers is an uphill battle. To begin with, older workers are often placed in the untenable position of competing with unemployed youth for the same jobs. Secondly, while mandatory retirement has essentially been removed in the United States, early retirement, often in the form of "golden handshakes," is frequently used as back-door means of getting rid of older workers.

Older women represent two protected classes of workers based upon the Employment Opportunity Act of 1967: females and over forty years old. According to the Age Discrimination in Employment Act (ADEA), workers cannot be demoted, transferred, or discharged based on age. Training and promotion cannot be denied because of age. Rather employers need to be mindful of affirmative action in designing and implementing training and promotion opportunities for qualified workers (Federal Glass Ceiling Commission, 1995).

Workers cannot be paid differently on the basis of age. One might further question whether it is fair being paid less working part time. Differential hourly wages, (as demonstrated in this research), based on differing hours of weekly work, can also be considered discriminatory, especially if the impact is primarily on certain categories of workers, such as older women.

Age cannot serve as the criteria for recruiting, hiring or refusing to hire new employees. Although legislation is in place to protect unfairly treated older workers, the reality is that most instances of age and sex discrimination go unnoticed or lose in court ("Cases involving Sex-and-Age Discrimination Against Midlife, Older Women Rarely Understood," August 1996. Filing a complaint or law suit usually requires a great deal of time and money; also, the employee often is at great risk of retaliation in the form of harassment, demotion, transfer, or job loss (Scott and Brudney, 1987). Because the Equal Employment Opportunity Commission is short staffed and inundated with cases, most cases are given inadequate attention that then forces individuals to file expensive, time-consuming lawsuits with a maximum pay-back ceiling of two years if the employer's violation was not willful and an added year if it was willful.

The Older Workers Benefit Protection Act (OWBPA), enacted on October 16, 1990, has restored ADEA's original prohibition against age discrimination regarding employee benefits. According to the law, reversed briefly in 1989 in the U.S. Supreme Court's Public Employees Retirement System of Ohio v. Betts (492 U.S. 158), employers cannot offer fewer benefits to older workers unless they can prove that the increased cost of the benefit increases with age (e.g., life insurance). Unfortunately, this condition for providing fewer benefits could backfire in the health care arena, especially with self-insured companies who might be able to document that older workers require additional health care costs.

Although educating employers about both the legal and human hazards of age discrimination is essential, legislation is not enough. If the expectation is that more older people work, then enormous efforts must be established in both the public and private arenas that address creation of jobs for seniors, job training opportunities, and alternative work schedules, especially part-time work. It is no wonder that non-working single older women from this research represent 5 1/2 times the working sample. There are few or no incentives to work, including adequate pay or employee benefits. In addition, there are many single older women who choose not to work in their later years.

The American Association of Retired Persons (AARP) has addressed the problem through its Worker Equity Initiative on behalf of older workers aimed at: (1) more jobs in the public and private sectors; (2) equal access to training and promotion; (3) more information about job protections and retirement options; (4) more services to elders in transition, who are entering the labor force for the first time, wanting a second career, or unemployed later in life; and (5) elimination of mandatory retirement on the basis of age (*The Age Discrimination in Employment Act Guarantees You Certain Rights*, AARP, p.8).

AARP has also been in partnership with the federal government in helping older workers rejoin the workforce. The Senior Community Service Employment Program (SCSEP) is a job placement service. Older job seekers sign up with SCSEP and are placed in host public or nonprofit organizations for short-term employment. In these sites they receive work experience, skills training, and job search education. AARP/SCSEP keeps thorough salary and performance records on all workers so that the most qualified can be referred for job interviews. Employers have access, without cost, to this pool of workers. In 1992, AARP/SCSEP, operating in 33 states and Puerto Rico, found jobs for 36 percent of its workforce—2096 older workers. SCSEP also operates a pilot program that pays the salary of workers placed in local private businesses. The employer agrees to hire a worker who successfully finishes a mutually agreed-upon training. In addition, job developers, who are also program participants, work with both employers and clients, matching the long-term workforce needs with the skills and interests of prospective workers. At the present time, AARP along with other sponsors offer 107 local SCSEP projects. In the first quarter of 1993 SCSEP was responsible for finding 789 jobs.

Contrary to strong negative opinion that results in job discrimination, there has been documented the perception of labor potential and talent among older workers. According to survey research administered to a large number of employees and supervisors by Yankelovich, Skelly, and White, Inc. (YSW) in 1985, older workers are appreciated especially for their knowledge, experience, attitudes, and work habits. Characteristics with ratings of excellent or very good by companies with 50-1,000+ employees include: (1) good attendance and punctuality; (2) commitment to quality; (3) loyalty and dedication to company; (4) a great deal of practical, not just theoretical, knowledge; (5) solid experience in job and/or industry; (6) solid/reliable performance record; (7) someone to count on in a crisis; (8) ability to get along with co-worker; and (9) emotional stability (*Workers Over 50: Old Myths, New Realities*, p. 7).

Gray Panthers, an all-volunteer advocacy group, has an age-discrimination-in-employment project. It has regular meetings for planning action and workshops for job seekers. In the spring of 1993 it held a public hearing on work problems and potential of workers over 45.

Companies that have been in the forefront of hiring initiatives for older workers as well as full utilization of existing older employees include Polaroid Corporation, Rockwell International, and Days Inn Corporation. Polaroid and Rockwell help retirees develop second careers as math and science teachers. Days Inn sponsors several Senior Job Fairs to recruit older workers.

In the public arena, two legislatively endorsed job training and placement programs have provided the financial and administrative support to economically disadvantaged persons who are 55 years of age and older. Title V, authorized under the Older Americans Act, has eligibility requirements of income, for an individual or couple, of no more than 125 percent of the amount determined as poverty level ($8,275 annual income for a single person as of July 1, 1991). Title V programs offer 20-hour-a-week jobs at minimum wage. Federal regulations mandate that these jobs add to local community service. A host agency must commit to giving first consideration to the intern if a vacancy occurs or if a new position is created that matches the intern's skills and experience.

The Job Partnership and Training Act Programs (JPTA) are the second of the two federally funded job training and placement programs for older adults. Income eligibility is established at 70 percent of the poverty line, but with inclusion of pensions and other money in the income calculation. In the Boston area, Operation ABLE (Ability Based on Long Experience) administers a JPTA program that is specifically focused on poor older minorities through the Older Minority Employment Initiative Program, one of several local and state organizations aimed at providing employment assistance (e.g., Massachusetts Department of Employment and Training, Jewish Vocational Services, Jobs for Older Bostonians, and Project Hire through the Arlington, MA Council on Aging). Most of these programs are partnerships using a variety of funds from both the private and public sectors (McKibben, 1992). Similarly supported programs exist throughout the country, requiring both matching funds and public/private endorsement. Unfortunately, a major issue in making available these programs to those most in need is the lack of widespread information. This problem of disseminating information about entitlements to eligible persons is universal; it is particularly evident with lesser known social supports, like Supplemental Security Income (Sohn, 1988). It is, therefore, important that a statewide system of information exists that includes publicity not only in employment sites but community facilities where the eligible population congregate, such as welfare agencies, municipal buildings, and even laundromats. Also, because JTPA targets its funds to different populations, the use of funds should be carefully monitored so that the appropriate level of funding is earmarked to aging workers, including older discouraged and unemployed workers and displaced homemakers.

Operation ABLE, a service organization in the Boston metropolitan area that promotes job placement, training (including computer skills), information and advocacy for people 45 years old and older, attacks the myths about older workers in its Older Worker National Campaign Packet ("Profitable Older Workers," 1990). According to Operation ABLE, the reality is: (1) creativity increases with age; (2) accident and attendance records are better for older than younger workers; (3) productivity levels for most occupations remains the same or better with age; (4) older workers have less stress at work and lower rates of psychiatric admissions than younger workers; (5) job satisfaction and maturity of older workers contribute to their interest and motivation to work; (6) adaptability is unrelated to age; and (7) there is a positive correlation between activity level and health, with enforced idleness contributing to deteriorating health.

In addition to general discrimination of older workers, what complicates the problem is more specific discrimination of part-time workers, which is probably the most viable work alternative for all older workers, including single older women. Hence, single older women are faced with double, if not triple (as females) jeopardy. Part-time workers are considered temporary, secondary wage earners, not serious about their careers or committed to labor force participation (Harriman, 1982; Jacobson, 1980; Meier, 1978; and Ronen, 1984). In fact, a pejorative term that is used to describe part-time workers is "disposable employees" ("The Changing Family to the Year 2000: Planning for Our Children's Future," 1987). Unlike full-time workers, part-time workers are assumed to be unhealthy, old or young, not eligible for promotions, not eligible for health insurance or retirement plans, most likely to be laid off, and marginal to the organization (Golden, 1987; Harriman, 1982).

Traditionally, labor unions have not supported part-time employment. Unions rarely represent part-time workers, who are perceived as threats to full-time workers. The fear is that part-time workers will replace full-time workers—at lower wages and with reduced or no benefits. In fact, some elements of the Women's Movement have voiced opposition to part-time work for similar reasons as unions; part-time work, as it exists now, leaves women with little or no economic power (Golden, 1987).

However, flexible work hours, including part-time employment, can offer a power base for women. "New Concept" part-time work, as described by Hilda Kahne (1985), takes into account varying hours of work for equitable pay (i.e., prorated, not less than full-time equivalent pay) *with* some career potential and benefits, primarily health insurance and employer-sponsored pensions. Unfortunately, most part-time jobs that exist today are in the retail trade and service industries in which the dual labor market patterns operate with low wages, no employee benefits, and little status (Cooperman, et. al., 1981; Nollen, 1978; Sheppard, and Mantovani, 1982). All these factors probably contribute to the fact that non-working single older women outnumber the working sample by 5 1/2 times, according to the SIPP data. If these women were given a real choice of working at jobs that include adequate pay, benefits, and flexible hours, there might be many more women opting to work, especially during economic times in which there is a surge in part-time employment opportunities.

One form of flexible work hours that seems to draw more acceptance from employers is job sharing, the division of one full-time job into two part-time positions that fulfill the responsibilities of the entire job. And, with increased likelihood of full-time equivalent pay, job sharing also may attract more older workers. (However, this research study can only determine numbers of part-time hours, not types of part-time jobs.) A survey of 238 job sharers demonstrated that they were valued for their increased flexibility, reduced absenteeism, increased productivity, and increased morale (Barrett, 1979; Meier, 1978). Through job sharing the employer is able to retain experienced employees that help to reduce recruitment and training costs and also can maintain a larger labor pool that partially supports a social solution to unemployment. On the negative side, job sharing and part-time work in general require more accountability, supervision, and record keeping (Meier, 1978; Nollen, 1982). According to Nollen, part-time employment necessitates an organizational climate that is less controlling, more informative, more employee-oriented, and more responsive to change rather than mechanistic and production-centered. Job sharing can also serve the purpose of phased retirement. Currently, most employees work full time and then suddenly retire without the economic, social, and emotional advantages of phasing in retirement through part-time work (Jondrow, 1983; Kahne, 1985). While phased retirement also allows the employer to hold on to valued employees, existing policy that determines the amount of both public and private pensions prevents the use of phased retirement. Public pensions are usually calculated from the last three consecutive years of highest earnings, which would be drastically reduced if hours of work were substantially dropped. Also, private pensions, if offered, are primarily determined by earnings. In order to encourage phased retirement, public policy and employment policy would have to offer new economic guidelines that do not penalize the part-time worker of less than 20 hours, such as in calculating the pension benefit on a prorated basis. In this way, the employee stays in the workforce maintaining an earnings income, continues to contribute to payroll and income taxes, and defers from collecting public or private pension benefits. This should offset the additional pension benefit amounts when full retirement is finally chosen. Another policy alternative could be offering a partial pension before phasing in retirement; by so doing, the employee would not be penalized for reduced hours and earnings and could even be eligible for additional pension benefits when fully retired.

As technology rapidly changes, all workers of all ages must be prepared to update their job skills through new training and education. The advantage of retraining older workers is that their experience, skills, and attitude are already company assets. In 1987, Aetna Life and Casualty of Hartford, Connecticut began to research the cost of replacement versus retention. It determined that replacement is very costly: approximately 93 percent of the first-year salary and benefits of the vacancy being filled. These costs are both direct and indirect and include recruitment (33%), training (10%), and time for moving up the learning curve (50%) for the new hire. A follow-up study 909 at Aetna determined that turnover of administrative and technical staff in 1989 cost almost $102 million (*Working Age*, May/June 1992, pp. 2-3). This is a convincing argument that retention of older workers is not only more humane but also much more cost-effective. Retaining these workers may require new kinds of training, such as programs in math, reading, and English as a second language and in computer software and hardware literacy.

For the single older woman who chooses to work full-time for financial or other reasons (e.g., social support, structure of daily life, professional satisfaction), flexible work hours can take the forms of flexitime or of compressed work weeks. There are variants of each, but essentially flexitime allows for flexible arrival and departure times with required work hours in between, and compressed work weeks permit the completion of full-time hours in less than five days per week. Flexitime is particularly attractive to the older woman worker who chooses to start or end work at nontraditional times based on lifestyle differences or conflicting commitments, such as caregiving responsibilities. Compressed work weeks, on the other hand, may be taxing on an older worker's energy level given the expanded work day; yet, this alternative work schedule provides a larger block of free time for leisure, caregiving, or anything else.

In summary, part-time employment offers both the worker and the workforce many advantages. The worker has the choice of greater job flexibility both in terms of total weekly hours and times of work. This flexibility accommodates the possibility of a changed lifestyle schedule, the conflicting demands of work and caregiving of aging relatives (Orodenker, 1988) and the choice of more leisure over labor (Harriman, 1987; "Exchanging Earnings for Leisure: Findings of an Exploratory National Survey on Work Time Preferences," 1980). Employment reforms can make creative use of all these assets and talents among older workers. They can take shape in a range of different forms that serve the purpose of encouraging elders to work, such as job training, retention and recruitment efforts, career development, legislation that supports affirmative action, family care, anti-discrimination measures, flexible work schedules of all kinds, and inclusion of employee benefits (primarily health insurance and private pensions) in job "packages." However, what is probably more important than any of these employment reforms is something more basic: prorated equitable pay based on hours of work. Whatever the personnel policies are that respond to aging workers' needs, it is recommended that they be formalized in writing, not left to the arbitrary decision making of individual supervisors (Mutschler and Miller, 1989).

INCOME ADEQUACY REFORMS

On average, single older working women are one step from poverty. As this research study demonstrates, their incomes are generally far from adequate, and their earnings barely keep them out of poverty. The reasons for their low economic status are related to shorter work histories (not analyzed in this study), lower wages and salaries, and less valued occupations in terms of both pay and prestige than those of most men. Also, they are much less likely to have private pension income that, along with savings and higher Social Security benefits, contributes significantly to well being in retirement.

If women were not relegated to a secondary segregated labor market, were paid comparable wages for relatively equal types of work, and had equal access to job-related retirement benefits, then they could consider the same choices of work versus leisure that men and married women have. Unfortunately, they are not treated the same or even comparably in the workforce and, therefore, cannot possibly entertain equivalent similar life choices.

Many single older women cannot work because of their health, physical limitations, or caregiving responsibilities to family members, primarily spouses and aging, disabled parents. Other single older women cannot work because the workplace has excluded them; there is no available employment because of a tight labor market, age discrimination, inflexible work hours and no part-time jobs. In other words, "for poor women, jobs are part of the problem as well as part of the solution" (p. 38, Tarr-Whelan and Crofton, eds., 1987).

Older women retire with meager Social Security benefits. In 1984, no working women in this research study received more than $5,000 annually to augment their total incomes. The three-legged stool of savings, private pensions, and Social Security that "cushion" many men in retirement is not available to most women. After retirement, these women survive solely on their meager Social Security. Given the way Social Security is calculated, women are penalized for their role of primary caregiver outside the labor force. Widows and never married women are least at risk for receiving the lowest Social Security; widows receive two-thirds of their deceased spouse's primary insurance amount (based upon his traditionally higher earnings), and white never married women have the advantage of higher Social Security from a longer tenure in covered employment (Loew, 1992). The older women most at risk for the lowest Social Security benefits are minorities, primarily blacks and Latinos, as well as divorcees who are entitled to one-half of her ex-spouse's benefit if the marriage lasted at least ten years.

The research findings of this study corroborate those of prior studies; among the different types of single older women, widows are most likely to have most non-earned income (including Social Security), and divorced women are most likely to have least. Never married women, in contrast, show more of a range of non-earned income.

How can the social adequacy be improved for these older women so that they can have some assurance of living beyond poverty and of being valued for their contribution to society by choosing to raise children? Alternative methods of calculating Social Security benefits serve the purpose of recognizing the value of caregiving work without pay and of reducing women's economic dependence on men. Earnings sharing gives credence to the rising labor force participation of women and to the interdependent relationship between spouses. It combines and divides the earnings credits acquired during marriage as well as the credits acquired outside marriage so that the calculated benefits represent more equitably women's contribution both to the family unit and to the workforce. For single older women, the actual amount of the benefit is determined with the death of a spouse for the widow or with divorce. With earnings sharing, divorced and widowed women would make use of their own earnings as well as their ex-spouses' earnings during the lifespan of the marriage. The resulting benefits for both groups of women would be more closely related to FICA taxes paid by the couples while married (Fierst, 1990). Divorced women would be assured of more adequate benefits and also would not have to remain married for at least ten years in order to be eligible for any benefit. Current law entitles divorced women to their ex-spouses' Social Security only if they had been married at least ten years, are retirement age themselves, and have Social Security earnings less than their ex-spouses'.

Earnings sharing plans change the balance between adequacy and equity, improving it for some and worsening it for others. For some, earnings sharing offers more equity because work (paid or unpaid) of both spouses during a marriage is credited towards Social Security. Also, earnings sharing may contribute to more adequacy, since those now making lower benefits would be entitled to more, and those making more benefits might be entitled to less. In fact, the proposal by the Technical Committee on Earnings Sharing would do just that—that is, increase the amounts to those with lower benefits and primarily decrease the amounts to those with higher benefits (Fierst, 1990). A 45-year phase-in period was recommended in order to minimize opposition from those who might suffer a loss with earnings sharing (Schulz, 1992). In practical terms, what this means is that workers as young as 45 years from retirement would have the choice of Social Security based on either their earnings sharing calculation or on their guaranteed fraction of their current law benefit, whichever is higher.

Another reform to Social Security could be changing the averaging period, so that forty work quarters are not required for eligibility. By so doing, women with short paid work histories due to caregiving of children earlier in life and of parents or spouses later in life would be financially compensated for their alternative work. The Childcare Dropout Years (CDY) policy allows the elimination of any year when there is a child under six and earnings are less than half of the national average wage (O'Grady, 1982). The result of this policy is to increase caregivers' PIAs (Primary Insurance Amounts) and thereby not penalize them for years of unpaid work which, if included in the Social Security calculation, would lower their PIAs.

The National Commission on Social Security has recommended a Modified Special Minimum Benefit that includes a maximum of ten childcare credit years. These years of no earnings when children were younger than six could be added to the total number of years of coverage. The other requirements without the additional modification of increased coverage years would still remain, specifically a minimum of ten years of work plus earnings of 25 percent or more of the maximum taxable amount. This policy would be targeted to those women with long, yet poorly paid, work histories who stop working in order to provide family care.

However, whether any of these policies address income adequacy for single older women is questionable (Loew, 1992; O'Grady, 1982). Provision of homemaker credits, as described above, will essentially benefit higher-income families (Holden, 1982). In addition to issues about the cost effectiveness and appropriate targeting of these policies, there is also much dispute about eligibility, accountability, and responsibility: who is eligible and how much credit should a homemaker receive, how does one assure accurate reporting of homemaker services, and under whose authority should decisions be made (Schulz, 1992)?

Eliminating—or liberalizing significantly—the earnings ceiling (or earnings test) on Social Security certainly could improve the income adequacy of single older working women. By so doing, the government would be offering another "carrot" to staying in the workforce. However, this incentive would only be made possible if there truly was a labor shortage and society wanted to increase the retirement age. Otherwise, Social Security is likely to *discourage* employment—or retirement—as a choice rather than a "stick."

CAREGIVING REFORMS

As described above, addressing the stress of caregiving on already stressed single older working women can be accomplished indirectly through employment reforms or policies for income adequacy. From this research study, one cannot determine specifically why so many single older women work part time or not at all. One speculation is that labor force demand is driven by employers, who are hiring more part-time, low paid workers. Another speculation is that workers, wanting more job flexibility, are influencing labor market supply. And, one reason for wanting more job flexibility is the increasing responsibility of caregiving among aging women workers.

Research from the National Long-Term Care Survey (NLTCS) demonstrates that in 1982 over 30 percent of the 2.2 million caregivers 65 years of age and older (660,000+) who were assisting 1.2 million frail elderly participated in the workforce. Yet, another 9 percent had to stop working in order to perform caregiving activities. Of those who remained in the labor force, about 20 percent decreased their working hours or took leave without pay, and almost 30 percent took advantage of alternative work schedules in order to caregive (Mutschler, 1990). Blue collar workers are more likely to suffer work loss, which results in major financial losses for workers and their families (Mutschler, 1989).

From this same survey is research related to the association between working and stress levels from caregiving (Giele, Mutschler, Orodenker, 1987; Orodenker, 1988; Mutschler, 1989a). The researchers determined that working per se does not necessarily contribute to stress. In fact, older, caregiving working women in the sample have much less stress than the non-working caregivers who previously or never worked. The working women who have good health, a network of informal caregiving supports, and separate living arrangements from their dependent elders, experience less stress than caregivers with physical problems, no shared caregiving, and shared households. What is more likely to exacerbate stress than working, according to Orodenker, are hours of caregiving, level of disability of the dependent elder, health status of the caregiver, and financial burdens of caregiving. Feelings of usefulness among the working women are the strongest predictor of stress level; the self perception of being valued by the dependent relative correlates with reduced stress.

Even more disabled than sample members of the NLTCS were study participants in the Channeling Experiment of the National Long-Term Care Demonstration (1984). Although one-third of the primary caregivers were working, mainly full time, at the time of the interview, one-third of those working had to limit their work hours. And, another 35 percent of caregivers recently employed had to leave work within the last year due to the heavy demands of their caregiving responsibilities.

These research findings point to several policy implications. Working in and of itself is not necessarily deleterious to the health and well being of older women. The findings in this study show that health problems account for only one percent of the part-time workforce and even less of the overall sample, inclusive of both part-time and full-time single older women. Hours of work, inflexibility of working hours, and lack of caregiving supports (both within the family and within the community) are probably more harmful than working itself. If the workforce and society at large are committed to encouraging labor force participation among older people, caregiving policies and practices must be put in place both by employers and by legislators. In addition to more widespread provision of alternative work schedules and part-time employment opportunities for older workers, described earlier as employment reforms, policies and programs specific to caregiving must be instituted in both the public and private sector. Information and referral programs at the work site are relatively easy to establish and cost effective. Work/Family Directions, a Boston area consulting firm that advises large businesses (e.g., IBM) on ways to help workers balance work and family life, has expanded its definition of dependent care and its original focus on child care to include the needs of employees' elderly parents. Besides its consulting function, Work/Family is now overseeing the American Business Collaboration for Quality Dependent Care, a group of 137 companies and organizations who are spending $26 million on community projects nationwide geared towards child and elder care.

The Travelers Insurance Company offers an extensive information program. Lunchtime seminars are held related to varying aspects (physically, mentally, emotionally, and financially) of family elder care. A peer support group for caregivers meets weekly. The Travelers also incorporates its commitment to caregiving in its employee benefit structure. Up to $5,000 of pre-taxed dollars can be set aside from their pay as their dependent care allowance; this money can be used to purchase caregiving for a dependent elderly family member (or child). In fact, forty percent of the companies surveyed by the Washington Business Group on Health (including Hallmark Cards, Proctor and Gamble, PepsiCo, TransAmerica, Champion, and Travelers) had flexible spending accounts permitting pretax contributions used for dependent care; the employees in half of these companies used them for eldercare (Mutschler and Miller, 1989).

Section 129 of the Internal Revenue Service Code has "win-win" provisions for both the employee and the employer; it allows for the exclusion of employer-provided dependent care benefits from an employee's gross income and for a deduction as a business expense from the employer's gross income.

Dependent care was originally directed exclusively towards the needs of young children and their families. As longevity increases and as more women are working and less available to caregive, dependent care becomes an issue at both ends of the age spectrum—for both young and old. Responsiveness to issues of dependent care can take the form of educational and information and referral programs, employee benefits (including family leave as well as pre-taxed elder care allowance), and community services such as adult day care and respite care. Family Leave legislation has recently been enacted to protect workers, usually women, who need to take time off following a pregnancy or adoption, but more liberally it is used to allow for extended care (up to three months) of a dependent child or elder parent. Family Leave legislation guarantees unpaid leave to employees of most businesses as well as a return to work at the same or similar level with retained employee benefits. Small businesses are the most outspoken opponents, because extended leaves with assured job returns are costly and can significantly contribute to bankruptcy.

HEALTH CARE REFORMS

If the data in this research suggests that many, if not most, single women under age 65 work mostly full time for access and payment of health insurance, then health care policies should offer a real *choice* of working full time, part time, or not at all. As designed by Hillary Rodman Clinton and the Commission she heads, universal health care available to all, on the job or unemployed, offers this possibility of real choice. Because "universal" health care is still a concept and not a reality, older women, as represented by the Older Women's League (OWL), are particularly concerned that health care services are comprehensive and affordable; inclusive of preexisting conditions, preventive tests such as mammograms and pap smears, and long-term care; and available to all who work (including those working part time) and who do not work.

It may be that many more women, who are currently either working full time or not at all, will choose to work part time. With universal health care, part-time workers, especially those working less than half time and employed in small businesses, may have equal access to health insurance. With universal health care, the employee of a small company is apt to benefit much more than the employer, especially the employer who has not provided benefits of any kind including health insurance to his/her workforce. And, as this study demonstrates, part-time employees, who traditionally have had few or no employee benefits, are more likely to work in these small businesses, which will be mandated to offer health insurance coverage with health care reform. On the other hand, the employer of a large firm with self insurance may have an advantage with health care reform, contributing less to a regional health alliance than current payments of employee health insurance.

However, it may be that with health care reform many more older women will choose not to work at all if their only incentive to working has been receiving health insurance. If all Americans have equal access to health insurance, whether or not they work, the motivation to work, particularly more hours, will be based on other factors, such as economics, social support, or job satisfaction.

The "fallout" from universal health care, unfortunately, may be shrinking of the labor force, reductions in salaries and hourly wages, and increasing age discrimination, all of which may further penalize the single older working woman who has relied on work for financial survival. Older workers in general may have less job security and may be increasingly offered early retirement packages, which will no longer require as an incentive the inclusion of retiree health care coverage.

On the other hand, Clinton's health reform may come as a blessing to some small employers who presently cannot afford to offer health insurance benefits to their employees. Under the new reform, small firms would join regional health alliances creating large buying pools for bargaining lower costs. Under Clinton's proposal, the contribution of a business of any size would be capped at 6.5 percent of payroll; any excess over that amount would be covered by small-business subsidies (Shao, Sept. 26, 1993). Thus, for some small businesses, most likely those that already provide health insurance coverage, the end result is positive and may lead to hiring more workers, full time and part time.

CONCLUSION

Single older working women cannot be considered or treated the same as married older working women, as single older non-working women, as single younger working women, and as single older working men. As women of advanced age who are making it on their own without the additional resources of men, they need public and private protection that pays attention to their employment, income, caregiving, and health care needs. As women, their "lifetime rhythms" (Kahne, 1985-86, p.11) and their investments in human capital are different from men's. As a result of these differences as well as occupational segregation in the secondary labor market (Giele,1978; Rogers, 1985), older women, particularly older single women, are at great risk for living in poverty. Public and private policies must be aimed at giving these women an opportunity to live with basic dignity, a floor of financial and health care protection, and choice about how to live their later years—working full time, part time, or not at all.

Bibliography

"AARP Supports Women's Pension Legislation—Says Small Reforms Make A Big Difference," 1996. AARP WebPlace, May 14, 1-2.

Achenbaum, W. Andrew, 1983. *Shades of Gray—Old Age, American Values, and Federal Policies Since 1920*. Boston: Little, Brown, and Co.

Age Discrimination on the Job, 1992. Washington, D.C.: American Association of Retired Persons.

Aging American: Trends and Projections (1987-1988 Edition). Washington, D.C.: United States Senate Special Committee on Aging.

America's Changing Work Force, 1993. Washington, D.C.: American Association of Retired Persons.

Anderson, Joseph. M., David L. Kennell, and John F. Sheils, Spring 1983. "Estimated Effects of 1983 Changes in Employer Health Plan/Medicare Payment Provisions on Employer Costs and Employment of Older Workers." (Research Report) Washington, D.C.: National Commission for Employment Policy.

Appelbaum, Eileen, 1987. "Restructuring Work: Temporary, Part-Time, and At-Home Employment." In Heidi I. Hartmann, ed., *Computer Chips and Paper Clips: Technology and Women's Employment*, Volume II (Case Studies and Policy Perspectives). Washington, D.C.: National Academy Press, 1987.

Axel, Helen, 1987. "Part-Time Employment: Crosscurrents of Change." Presentation at Conference on The Contingent Workplace: New Directions for Work in the Year 2000, January 15-16, New York.

Barker, Kathleen, 1993. "Changing Assumptions and Contingent Solutions: The Cost and Benefits of Women Working Full-Time and Part-Time." *Sex Roles* 28 (Number 1/2): 47-71.

Barrett, N.S., 1979. "Women in the Job Market: Unemployment and Work Schedules." In Robert Smith, ed., *The Subtle Revolution: Women at Work*. Washington, D.C.: The Urban Institute.

Belous, Richard S., 1989. *The Contingent Economy: The Growth of the Temporary, Part-Time and Subcontracted Workforce.* Washington, D.C.: National Planning Association.

Benefits for Part-Time Employees, 1985. Lincolnshire, IL: Hewitt Associates.

Birren, James E., Pauline K. Robinson, and Judy E. Livingston, eds.,1986. *Age, Health, and Employment.* Englewood Cliffs, NJ: Prentice-Hall.

Binstock, Robert H., 1985. *Handbook of Aging and the Social Sciences.* New York: Van Nostrand and Reinhold Co.

Binstock, Robert H. and Stephen G. Post, 1991. *Too Old for Health Care.* Baltimore: The Johns Hopkins University Press.

Blank, Rebecca M., July 1985. "Simultaneously Modelling The Supply of Weeks and Hours of Work Among Female Household Heads." Princeton, NJ: Princeton University.

_____, 1986. "Part-Time Work and Wages Among Adult Women." Presentation at the Industrial Relations Research Association Meetings, December, New Orleans.

_____, 1988. "The Role of Part-Time Work in Women's Labor Market Choices Over Time." Conference Presentation Sponsored by the Committee on the Status of Women in the Economic Profession. (November).

_____, 1990. "Are Part-Time Jobs Bad Jobs?" In Gary Burtless, ed., *A Future of Lousy Jobs?* Washington, D.C.: The Brookings Institution, 123-164.

Bluestone, Barry and Bennett Harrison, 1986. "The Great American Job Machine: The Proliferation of Low Wage Employment in the U.S. Economy." Study Prepared for the Joint Economic Committee. (December).

Blyton, Paul, 1985. *Changes in Working Time—An International Review.* New York: St. Martin's Press.

Boaz, Rachel F., 1987. "Working as a Response to Low and Decreasing Real Income During Retirement." *Research on Aging,* 9 (September): 428-440.

Bowen, W.G. and T.A. Finegan, 1969. *The Economics of Labor Force Participation.* Princeton, NJ: Princeton University Press.

Brody, S. J., 1976. "Public Policy Issues of Women inTransition." *Gerontologist,* 16 (2): 181-183.

Brown, Diane R.,1988. "Employment and Health Among Older Black Women: Implications for Their Economic Status." Presentation for Conference on Older Minority Women at Wellesley College, Center for Research on Women, March 22.

Burkhauser, Richard V. and Robert H. Haveman, 1982. *Disability and Work—The Economics of American Policy*. Baltimore: The Johns Hopkins University Press.

Butler, Robert N. and Herbert P. Gleason, eds., 1985. *Productive Aging—Enhancing Vitality in Later Life*. New York: Springer Publishing.

Cain, Glen C., 1976. "The Challenge of Segmented Labor Market Theories to Orthodox Theory: A Survey." *Journal of Economic Literature*, (December 9): 1215-57.

Campione, Wendy A., 1987. "The Married Woman's Retirement Decision: A Methodological Comparison." *Journal of Gerontology*. 2 (Number 4): 381-386.

"Cases Involving Sex-and-Age Discrimination Against Midlife, Older Women Rarely Understood, 1996." AARP WebPlace, August 6 1-2.

Chakravarty, S. and K. Weisman, Nov. 14, 1988. "Consuming Our Children?," *Forbes*, 282-232.

Chan, T. and D. Fowles, 1980. *The Older Worker: Statistical Reports on Older Americans*. Washington, D.C.: Government Printing Office.

The Changing Workplace: New Directions in Staffing and Scheduling, 1986. (Bureau of National Affairs Special Report) Washington, D.C.: Bureau of National Affairs.

Christensen, Kathleen, 1987. "Women and Contingent Work." *Social Policy*. (Spring): 15-18.

Cieck, James, Seth Epstein and Jerry Goldman, 1995. "Updated Estimates of Work-Life Expectancies Based upon the Increment-Decrement Model." *Journal of Legal Economics* 5 (1), Spring-Summer, 1-33.

Cirilli, Mary and Diane Lindner, et. al., Dec. 1981. *Pre-Retirement Work Options—Final Report—Project Implementation*, Volume I. Madison, Wisconsin: State of Wisconsin, Department of Employment Relations, Division of Human Resource Services.

Claman, Priscilla H., 1979. *It Works: Part-Time Employment in State Agencies*. Boston: Commonwealth of Massachusetts, Executive Office for Administration and Finance, Division of Personnel Administration.

Clark, Robert L. and Joseph J. Spengler, 1980. *The Economics of Individual and Population Aging*. New York: Cambridge University Press.

Clark, Robert L. and David T. Barker, 1981. *Reversing the Trend Toward Early Retirement*. Washington, D.C.: American Institute for Public Policy Research.

Clark, Robert L., 1983. "Sources of Labor Market Problems of Older Persons Who Are Also Women, Handicapped, and/or Members of Minority Groups." (Research Report) Washington, D.C.: National Commission for Employment Policy.

Clark, Robert L., George L. Maddox, Ronald A. Schrimper, and Daniel A. Sumner, 1984. *Inflation and the Economic Well-Being of the Elderly.* Baltimore: Johns Hopkins Press.

Cooperman, Lois F., Fred D. Keast, and Douglas G. Montgomery, 1981. "Older Workers and Part-Time Work Schedules." *Personnel Administrator* (October): 35-38.

Crittenden, Ann, 1994. "Temporary Solutions." *Working Woman* (February): 32-35+.

Crown, William H., 1985. "Some Thoughts on Reformulating the Dependency Ratio." *The Gerontologist,* 25 (Number 2): 166-171.

_____, April 1989. "Policy Alternatives for Facilitating Employment of Older Persons." Waltham, MA: Policy Center on Aging, Heller School, Brandeis University.

_____,1990. "Economic Trends, Politics, and Employment Policy for Older Workers," *Journal of Aging and Social Policy,* Vol. 2 (3/4), 131-151.

Crown, William H., Phyllis H. Mutschler, and Thomas Leavitt, 1987. "Characteristics of Older Workers and The Implications for Employment Policy." Waltham, MA: Heller School, Brandeis University, The Policy Center on Aging.

Crown, William H., Phyllis H. Mutschler, James H. Schulz, and Rebecca Loew, 1993. "The Economic Status of Divorced Older Women." Waltham, MA: Policy Center on Aging, Heller School, Brandeis University.

Davis, Richard H., ed., 1981. *Aging: Prospects and Issues.* Los Angeles: University of Southern California Press.

Dennis, Helen, 1984. *Retirement Preparation.* Lexington, MA: Lexington Books.

Doering, Mildred, Susan R. Rhodes, and Michael Schuster, 1983. *The Aging Worker—Research and Recommendations.* Beverly Hills: Sage.

Doress, Paula B. and Diana L. Siegal, et. al., 1987. *Ourselves, Growing Older.* New York: Simon and Schuster.

duRivage, Virginia, 1986. *Working at the Margins: Part-Time and Temporary Workers in the United States.* Cleveland: National Association of Working Women.

_____, ed., 1992. *New Policies for the Part-Time and Contingent Workforce.* Armonk, NY: M.E. Sharpe.

Ehrenberg, Ronald G., Pamela Rosenberg, and Jeanne Li, 1986. "Part-Time Employment in the United States." Presentation at Conference on Employment, Unemployment, and Hours of Work, Berlin, Germany, Sept. 17-19.

Eller, T.J., June 1996. "Who Stays Poor? Who Doesn't?" *Current Population Reports*, Census Bureau, U.S. Dept. of Commerce, Economics and Statistics Administration, 1-6.

Employee Benefit Research Institute Notes, 1993. Washington, D.C.: EBRI Education and Research Fund 14 (Number 12): 1-12.

Exchanging Earnings for Leisure: Findings of an Exploratory National Survey on Work Time Preferences, 1978. (Research and Development Monograph 79) Washington, D.C.: Employment and Training Administration, United States Department of Labor.

Eyde, Lorraine D., 1975. *Flexibility Through Part-Time Employment of Career Workers in the Public Service*. Washington, D.C.: United States Civil Service Commission, Personnel and Development Center.

Federal Glass Ceiling Commission, November 1995. *Solid Investment: Making Full Use of the Nation's Human Capital.* Washington D.C.: Government Printing Office.

Ferber, Marianne H. and Brigid O'Farrell, eds., 1991. *Work and Family: Policies for a Changing Work Force*. Washington, D.C.: National Academy Press.

Fields, Gary S. and Olivia S. Mitchell, 1983. "Restructuring Social Security: How Well Retirement Ages Respond?" (Research Report) Washington, D.C.: National Commission for Employment Policy.

Fleisher, Dorothy, 1981. "Alternative Work Options for Older Workers: Part IV—Policy Implications." *Aging and Work* (Summer): 153-160.

"Flexible Work Schedules," 1973. (A Catalyst Position Paper) New York: Catalyst.

Focus Your Future: A Woman's Guide to Retirement Planning, 1991. Washington, D.C.: American Association of Retired Persons.

Fox, Alan, 1984. "Income Changes At and After Social Security Benefit Receipt: Evidence From the Retirement History Study." *Social Security Bulletin*, 47, (September): 3-23.

Fox, Mary F. and Sharlene Hesse-Biber, 1984. *Women at Work*. California: Mayfield Publishing.

Fraser, Irene, 1988. *Promoting Health Insurance in the Workplace: State and Local Initiatives to Increase Private Coverage*. Chicago: American Hospital Association.

Fullerton, H., 1985. "The 1995 Labor Force: BLS' Latest Projections," *Monthly Labor Review*, 108 (11), 17-25.

The Future of Older Workers in America. New Options for an Extended Working Life, 1980. Scarsdale, New York: Work in America Institute.

Gibeau, Janice L., 1986. "Breadwinners and Caregivers: Working Patterns of Women Working Full Time and Caring for Dependent Elderly Family Members." Ph.D. Dissertation. Waltham, MA: Heller School, Brandeis University.

Giele, Janet Z., 1978. *Women and the Future*. New York: Free Press.

Giele, Janet Z. and Mary Gilfus, 1990. "Race and College Differences in Life Patterns of Educated Women." In Joyce Antler and Sari Biklen, eds., *Women and Educational Change*. Albany: SUNY Press, 179-197.

Giele, Janet Z., Phyllis H. Mutschler, and Sylvia Z. Orodenker, Jan. 1987. "Stress and Burdens of Caregiving for the Frail Elderly," Working Paper #36. Waltham, MA: Policy Center on Aging, Heller School, Brandeis University.

Gist, John R., 1988. "The Impact of Tax Reform on Low Income Older Women." Washington, D.C.: American Association of Retired Persons, Public Policy Institute.

Gohmann, Stephan F., "Retirement Differences Among the Respondents to the Retirement History Survey," *Journal of Gerontology: Social Sciences* 45 (3), May, 120-127.

Golden, Lonnie, 1987. *Social Insecurity: The Economic Marginalization of Older Workers*. Cleveland: National Association of Working Women.

Gollub, James O., 1983. "Emerging Employment Options for Older Workers: Practice and Potential." (Research Report) Washington, D.C.: National Commission for Employment Policy.

Gorov, Lynda, Sept. 29, 1985. "Juicy Incentives, Mixed Results."

Gustman, Alan L. and Thomas L. Steinmeier, 1985. "The Effect of of Partial Retirement on the Wage Profiles of Older Workers." *Industrial Relations* 24 (Spring): 257-265.

Hammond, D., 1986. "Health Care for Old Women: Curing the Disease." In M. J. Bell, ed., *Women as Elders: Images, Visions, and Issues*. New York: Haworth Press.

Hanlon, Martin D., 1986. "Age and Commitment to Work." *Research on Aging*, 8 (June): 289-316.

Hanoch, Giora and Marjorie Honig, 1993. "Retirement, Wages, and Labor Supply of the Elderly." *Journal of Labor Economics*, 1 (2), April, 131-151.

Harriman, Ann, 1982. *The Work/Leisure Trade Off—Reduced Work Time for Managers and Professionals.* New York: Praeger.

Health Benefits for an Aging Workforce: Issues and Strategies, 1988. Washington, D.C.: Washington Business Group on Health, Institute on Aging, Work, and Health and American and Association of Retired Persons, Worker Equity Initiative.

Herz, Diane E.,1988. "Employment Characteristics of Older Women, 1987." *Monthly Labor Review* (Sept.) 111, 3-12.

Herz, Diane E. and Philip L. Rones, 1989. "Institutional Barriers to Employment of Older Workers." *Monthly Labor Review*, 112 (April): 14-21.

Holden, Karen C., 1982. "Supplemental OASI Benefits to Homemakers through Current Spouse Benefits, a Homemaker Credit, and Child-Care Drop-Out Years." In R.V. Burkhauser and K.C. Holden, *A Challenge to Social Security.* New York: Academic Press, 41-65.

Holden, Karen C. and Timothy W. Bosworth, 1981. "Pre-Retirement Work Options: Evaluation Report," Volume 2.

Iams, Howard M., 1985. "Characteristics of the Longest Job for New Retired Workers: Findings From The New Beneficiary Survey." *Social Security Bulletin* 48 (March): 5-14.

_____, 1986a. "Employment of Retired-Worker Women." *Social Security Bulletin* (March): 5-13.

_____, 1986b. "Transition to Retirement Jobs." Presentation to the Annual Meetings of the Gerontological Society of America, Chicago, November 18.

_____, 1987. "Jobs of Persons Working After Receiving Retired-Worker Benefits." *Social Security Bulletin* 50 (November): 4-18.

Irick, Christine, 1985. "Income of New Retired Workers by Social Security Benefit Levels: Findings From The New Beneficiary Survey." *Social Security Bulletin* 48 (May).

Jacobson, Beverly, 1980. *Young Programs for Older Workers—Case Studies in Progressive Personnel Policies.* New York: Van Nostrand Reinhold.

Jondrow, James M., Frank Brechling, and Alan Marcus, 1983. "Older Workers in the Market for Part-Time Employment." (Professional Paper 396) Alexandria, Virginia: The Public Policy Research Institute.

Kahne, Hilda, 1979. "Women's Occupational Choices and Lifetime Work Rhythms: Are We Still Making Progress?" *Journal of Employment Counseling* 16 (June) 83-93.

_____, 1981. "Economic Security of Older Women: Too Little for Too Late in Life." Waltham, MA: Brandeis University, Policy Center on Aging.

_____, 1985. *Reconceiving Part-Time Work—New Perspectives for Older Workers and Women.* Totowa, NJ: Rowman and Allanheld.

_____, 1985-86. "Not Yet Equal: Employment Expeiences of Older Women and Older Men," *International Journal on Aging and Human Development,* Vol. 22 (1), 1-13.

_____, 1986. "Part-Time Work: A Positive Case." Presentation at Industrial Relations Research Association Annual Meetings, New Orleans, December 30.

_____, 1992. "Part-Time Work: A Hope and a Peril." In Barbara Warme, Katherina L. P. Lundy and Larry A. Lundy, eds., *Working Part-Time: Risks and Opportunities.* New York: Praeger.

_____, 1993. "Part-Time Work: A Reassessment for a Changing Economy" (Draft). Waltham, MA: Heller School, Brandeis University.

Kahne, Hilda and Janet Z. Giele, eds., 1992. *Women's Work and Women's Lives: Continuing Struggle Worldwide.* Bolder, CO: Westview Press.

Kaplan, Barbara H., 1981."Alternative Work Options For Older Workers: Part III—The Union and Professional Association View." *Aging and Work* (Summer): 146-152.

Kaplan, Barbara, 1984. "Women 65 and Over: Factors Associated with Their Decision to Work." Ph.D. Dissertation. Waltham, MA: Heller School, Brandeis University.

Kingson, Eric R. "Men Who Leave Work Before Age 62: A Study of Advantaged and Disadvantaged Very Early Labor Force Withdrawal." Ph.D. Dissertation. Waltham, MA: Heller School, Brandeis University.

Kingson, Eric R. and Barbara A. Hirshhorn, and John M. Cornman, 1986. *Ties that Bind.* Washington, D.C.: Seven Locks Press.

Kingson, Eric R. and Regina O'Grady-Le Shane, 1993. "The Effects of Caregiving on Women's Social Security Benefits." *The Gerontologist* 33 (Number 2): 230-39.

Kohen, Andrew I., 1983. "Multiple Liability? A Survey and Synthesis of Research Literature Pertaining to Labor Market Problems of Selected Groups of Older Workers." Washington, D.C.: National Commission for Employment Policy.

Kotlikoff, Laurence J., 1993. *Generational Accounting.* New York: The Free Press.

Leon, C. and R. Bednarzik, 1978. "A Profile of Women on Part-Time Schedules." *Monthly Labor Review* 10 (Number 10): 3-12.

Leontief, Wassily, Nov. 7, 1983. *Business Week*, 16.

Levitan, Sara A. and Elizabeth A. Conway, 1988. "Part-Timers: Living on Half Rations." *Challenge* 31 (Number 3): 9-16.

Levitan, Sara A. and Isaac Shapiro, 1987. "What's Missing in Welfare Reform?" *Challenge* 30 (July-August): 44-48.

"Life Cycle Planning. New Strategies for Education, Work, and Retirement in America," Summary of National Conference, April 20-22, 1977. Washington, D.C.: Center for Policy Process.

Loew, Rebecca M., 1992. "Determinants of Divorced Older Women's Labor Force Participation." Ph. D. Dissertation. Waltham, MA: Heller School, Brandeis University.

Longman, Phillip, 1985. "Justice Between Generations." *The Atlantic Monthly* (June): 73-81.

Loth, Renee, 1986. "Where's The Grace in Growing Old?" *The Boston Globe Magazine*, June 8, 16-20+.

Markson, Elizabeth W., ed., 1983. *Older Women—Issues and Prospects*. Lexington, MA: Lexington Books.

Maxfield, Linda D. and Virginia P. Reno, 1985. "Distribution of Income Sources of Recent Retirees: Findings From The New Beneficiary Survey." *Social Security Bulletin* 48 (January): 7-13.

McBride, Timothy D., 1988. "The Retirement Behavior of Women: Findings from the 1982 New Beneficiary Survey." Washington, D.C.: The Urban Institute.

McConnell, Stephen R., 1981. "Alternative Work Options for Older Workers: Part II—The Managers' View." *Aging and Work* (Spring): 81-87.

McKibben, Margaret, May 1992. *Opportunities for Older People— Volunteer Work and Employment Resources*. Boston: Gerontology Institute, University of Massachusetts at Boston.

Meier, Elizabeth L., 1986. "Employment Experience and Income of Older Women." Washington, D.C.: American Association of Retired Persons, Public Policy Institute.

Meier, Gretl S., 1978. *Job Sharing—A New Pattern for Quality of Work and Life*. Kalamazoo, MI: W.E. Upjohn Institute for Employment Research.

Meltz, Noah M., Frank Reid, and Gerald S. Swartz, 1981. *Sharing the Work: An Analysis of the Issues in Worksharing and Job Sharing*. Buffalo: University of Toronto.

Mutschler, Phyllis H., Nov. 1989a. "Eldercare and the Collar Connection: Occupation and Work Constraints," Working Paper #52. Waltham, MA: Policy Center on Aging, Heller School.

_____, Dec. 1989b. "Disrupted Employment among Caregivers to Frail Elders," Working Paper #48. Waltham, MA: Policy Center on Aging, Heller School, Brandeis University.

_____, Feb. 1990. "New Efforts to Meet the Nees of Working Caregivers." *Of Current Interest.* (Brandeis University Policy Center on Aging Newsletter), 9, 4-5.

Mutschler, Phyllis H. and Judith R. Miller, 1989. "Eldercare: An Issues Overview" (Part 3). In *1990 Supplement of the Sourcebook on Post-Retirement Health Care Benefits,* ed. by Diane Disney. New York: Panel Publishers, Inc.

Myles, John, 1984. *Old Age in the Welfare State.* Boston: Little, Brown, and Company.

Nardone, Thomas J., 1986. "Part-Time Workers: Who Are They?" *Monthly Labor Review* (February): 13-19.

Nollen, Stanley D., Brenda B. Eddy, and Virginia H. Martin, 1978. *Permanent Part-Time Employment—The Manager's Perspective.* New York: Praeger.

Nollen, Stanley D., 1982. *New Work Schedules in Practice—Managing Time in a Changing Society.* New York: Van Nostrand Reinhold.

O'Meara, Mary, 1971. "Part-Time Social Workers in Public Welfare." New York: Catalyst.

O'Rand, Angela M. and John C. Henretta, 1982. "Delayed Career Entry, Industrial Pension Structure, and Early Retirement in a Cohort of Unmarried Women." *American Sociological Review* 47 (June): 365-373.

O'Rand, Angela M., 1986. "The Hidden Payroll: Employee Benefits and the Structure of Workplace Inequality." *Sociological Forum* 1 (Number 4): 657-683.

O'Rand, Angela M. and Richard Landerman, 1988. "Women's and Men's Retirement Income Status." *Research on Aging* 6 (March): 25-44.

Older Americans in the Workforce. Challenges and Solutions (Bureau of National Affairs Special Report), 1987. Washington, D.C.: Bureau of National Affairs.

"Older Worker Project Delivers Jobs to Oklahoma Seniors," 1987. *Aging* (September) 26-27.

Older Workers: Prospects, Problems, and Policies, 1985. (9th Annual Report, Number 17). Washington, D.C.: National Commission for Employment Policy.

On the Other Side of Easy Street—Myths and Facts About the Economic Old Age, 1987. Washington, D.C.: The Villers Foundation.

Onyx, Jenny and Pam Benton, 1996. "Retirement: A Problematic Concept for Older Women." *Journal of Women & Aging* 8 (2), 19-34.

Orodenker, Sylvia Z., 1988. "The Effects of Women's Labor Force Participation on Levels of Stress Associated with the Caregiving Experience." Ph. D. Dissertation. Waltham, MA: Heller School, Brandeis University.

Owen, John D., 1979. *Working Hours. An Economic Analysis.* Lexington, MA: Lexington Books.

Parnes, Herbert S., ed., 1983. *Policy Issues in Work and Retirement.* Kalamazoo, Michigan: W.E. Upjohn Institute for Employment Research.

Pearldaughter, Andra, Virginia Dean, Frances Leonard and Tish Sommers, 1980. "Welfare: End of the Line for Women." (Gray Paper Number 5, Issues for Action) Washington, D.C.: Older Women's League, May 1-20.

Perkins, Kathleen, 1994. "Older Women in the Workplace and Implications for Retirement: EAP Can Make a Difference." *Employee Assistance Quarterly* 9 (3-4), 81-97.

Piacentini, Joseph S. and Timothy J. Cerino, 1990. *EBRI Databook on Employee Benefits.* Washington, D.C.: Employee Benefits Research Institute.

Platt, Bill, 1988. "Retirees Serve as Mentors to Young Offenders." *Aging* (Number 357), 14-16.

Polivka, Anne E. and Thomas Nardone, 1989. "On the Definition of 'Contingent' Work." *Monthly Labor Review* 112 (Number 3): 9-16.

Pollack, J., 1955. "Economic Gains from Continued Employment." In W. Donohue, ed., *Earning Opportunities for Older Workers.* Ann Arbor, MI: University of Michigan Press.

Retirement Income: 1984 Pension Law Will Help Some Widows but Not the Poorest, 1988. (Report to Congressional Committees) Washington, D.C.: United States General Accounting Office.

Returning to the Job Market: A Woman's Guide to Employment Planning, 1992. Washington, D.C.: American Association of Retired Persons.

Rogers, Gayle Thompson, 1985. "Nonmarried Women Approaching Retirement: Who Are They and When Do They Retire?." In *Current Perspectives on Aging and the Life Cycle*, Vol. 1. Greenwich, CT: Jai Press Inc.

Ronen, Simcha, 1984. *Alternative Work Schedules: Selecting...
Implementing...and Evaluating.* Homewood, IL: Dow-Jones-
Irwin.

Root, Lawrence S. and Laura H. Zarrugh, 1983. "Innovative
Employment Practices for Older Americans." (Research Report)
Washington, D.C.: National Commission for Employment
Policy.

Rothberg, Diane S. and Barbara E. Cook, 1987. *Employee Benefits for
Part-Timers,* Second Edition. Alexandria, VA: Association of
Part-Time Professionals.

Ruggles, Patricia, 1987. "The Economic Status of the Low-Income
Elderly: New Evidence from the SIPP." Presentation at the
Annual Meetings of the Gerontological Society, Washington,
D.C., November 20.

Rupp, Kalman, Edward C. Bryant, and Richard E. Mantovani, 1983.
"Factors Affecting the Participation of Older Americans in
Employment and Training Programs." (Research Report)
Washington, D.C.: National Commission for Employment
Policy.

Sandell, Steven H., ed., 1987. *The Problem Isn't Age.* New York:
Praeger.

Schofield, Rosalie F., 1984. "The Private Pension Coverage of Part-
Time Workers." Ph.D. Dissertation. Waltham, MA: Heller
School, Brandeis University.

Schulz, James H., 1988. *The Economics of Aging* (Fourth Edition).
Dover, MA: Auburn House.

_____, 1992. *The Economics of Aging* (Fifth Edition). New
York: Auburn House.

_____, 1986. "Social Security and Women." Presentation at
the American Association of Retired Persons Conference: United
States/Canada Expert Meeting on Policies for Midlife and Older
Women, October 16.

_____, "Job Matching in an Aging Society: Barriers to the
Utilization of Older Workers."

Schuster, Michael and Joan A. Kaspin, 1987. "The Age Discrimination
in Employment Act: An Evaluation of Federal and State
Enforcement, Employer Compliance and Employee
Characteristics." Final Report to the NRTA-AARP Andrus
Foundation.

Schuster, Michael and Christopher Miller, 1984. "An Empirical
Assessment of the Age Discrimination in Employment Act."
Industrial Labor Relations Review, 38 (1): 64-74.

Scott, Hilda and Juliet F. Brudney, 1987. *Forced Out*. New York: Simon and Schuster.

Shao, Maria, Sept. 26, 1993. "The Clinton Plan: How It Would Affect 3 Employers," *Boston Sunday Globe*, 53-54.

_____, Oct. 6, 1993. "Balancing More Than The Books," *Boston Globe*, 45+.

_____, April 3, 1994. "New U.S. Workers: Flexible, Disposable." *Boston Sunday Globe*, 1,18.

_____, April 3, 1994. "In Cambridge, New Take on Temps." *Boston Sunday Globe*, 18.

Shaw, Lois B., 1985. *Older Women at Work*. Washington, D.C.: Women's Research and Education Institute.

Sheppard, Harold L. and Sara E. Rix, 1977. *The Graying of Working America*. New York: Free Press.

Sheppard, Harold L. and Richard E. Mantovani, 1982. *Aging in the 80's: Part-Time Employment After Retirement*. (A Report for the Travelers Insurance Companies) Washington, D.C.: National Council on Aging.

A Single Person's Guide to Retirement Planning, 1990. Washington, D.C.: American Association of Retired Persons.

Smith, Shirley J., 1987. "Work Experience of the Labor Force During 1985." *Monthly Labor Review* 110 (Number 4): 40-44.

Sohn, Kisang, 1988. "A Study of the Economic Status of the Low-Induced Elderly: Who They Are and How They Fare." Ph.D. Dissertation. Waltham, MA: Heller School, Brandeis University.

Spalter-Roth and Heidi Hartmann, 1992. "Exploring the Characteristics of Self employment and Part-Time Work among Women" (Final Draft). Washington, D.C.: Institute of Women's Policy Research.

"Statement of the Older Women's League on Older Women and the Labor Force," 1984, Joint Economics Committee, Washington, D.C., June 6.

Stentzel, Cathy, 1987. *Women, Work and Age: A Report on Older Women and Employment*. Washington, D.C.: National Commission on Working Women.

Stolz, Barbara A.,1985. *Still Struggling—America's Low-Income Working Women Confronting the 80's*. Lexington, MA: Lexington Books.

Su, B., 1985. "The Economic Outlook to 1995: New Assumptions and Projections," *Monthly Labor Review*, 108 (11), 3-16.

Szinovacz, Maximiliane E., 1983. "Beyond the Hearth: Older Women and Retirement." In Elizabeth W. Markson, ed., *Older Women*. Lexington, MA: Lexington Books.

Tilly, Chris, 1991. "Reasons for the Continuing Growth of Part-Time Employment." *Monthly Labor Review* 114 (Number 3): 10-18.

U.S. Department of Labor, 1980. *Perspectives on Working Women: A Databook.* Washington, D.C.: Government Printing Office.

——————, Women's Bureau, September 1996. *Twenty Facts on Women Workers.* Washington D.C.: Government Printing Office.

Usher, Carolyn E., 1981. "Alternative Work Options for Older Workers: Part I—Employees' Interest." *Aging and Work* (Spring): 74-80.

Vanished Dreams: Age Discrimination and the Older Women Worker, 1980. Cleveland: National Association of Office Workers.

Viscusi, W. Kip., 1979. *Welfare of the Elderly: An Economic Analysis and Policy Prescription.* New York: John Wiley and Sons.

Waite, L., 1981. *U.S. Women at Work.* Santa Monica, CA: Rand Corporation.

Warlick, Jennifer, 1985. "Why is Poverty after 65 A Woman's Problem?" *Journal of Gerontology,* 40 (Number 6), 751-757.

Weaver, David A., 1994. "The Work and Retirement Decisions of Older Women: A Literature Review." *Social Security Bulletin* 57 (1), Spring, 3-24.

Weiss, Francine K., 1984. *Older Women and Job Discrimination: A Primer.* Washington, D.C.: Older Women's League.

A Woman's Guide to Pension Rights, 1992. Washington, D.C.: American Association of Retired Persons.

"Women and Social Security," 1985. *Social Security Bulletin* 48 (February).

Work and Retirement: Options for Continued Employment of Older Workers, 1982. Washington, D.C.: The Congress of the United States, Congressional Budget Office.

Work in America Institute, Inc.,1980. *The Future of Older Workers in America: New Options for Extended Working Life.* Scarsdale, N.Y. : Author.

Workers 45+: Today and Tomorrow, 1986. Washington, D.C.: American Association of Retired Persons.

Workers Over 50: Old Myths, New Realities, 1986. Washington, D.C.: American Association of Retired Persons.

Zola, Irving K., Oct. 5-6, 1987. "A 'Healthy' Public Policy for People with Disabilities." Presentation at The Healthy Public Policy Symposium, Yale University School of Medicine, New Haven, CT.

Index